...AND EGYPT
IS THE RIVER

...AND EGYPT IS THE RIVER

Michael S. Judge

SKYLIGHT PRESS

First published in Great Britain in 2013 by Skylight Press,
210 Brooklyn Road, Cheltenham, Glos GL51 8EA

Designed and typeset by Rebsie Fairholm
Publisher: Daniel Staniforth
Cover image: *Angelus Novus* by Paul Klee

www.skylightpress.co.uk

Printed and bound in Great Britain by Lightning Source, Milton Keynes.
Typeset in Vulpa, a font by Schizotype.

British Library Cataloguing-in-Publication data:
A catalogue record for this book is available from the British Library.

ISBN 978-1-908011-27-5

Thanks:

to mom, dad, Matthew, & Paul
to Molly
to Natalie
to Katie

to James Chapman & Carah Naseem

to Daniel, Rebsie, & everyone at Skylight

to the doctors: Marshall & Deborah Armintor, Ian Finseth,
Walton Muyumba, Dale Wilkerson, and Scott Simpkins (r.i.p.)

to Courtney & Conor
to Dylan, Maren, & Andy

to Matthew Remski

to Iain Sinclair, Brian Catling, Pierre Joris, & Jonathan Lethem

MSJ: September 2013

A. *Trouble. The beginning of chemistry. A type of explosion, or a way to sift explosions into classes. A way to freeze explosions in a row of bell-jars and walk down the row until you've learned to read them. The rip and hell of continents colliding. The letters that the continents churn up from their new muddy seam.*

How many voices came to them?

To Hibou, crouched with owl-lamps in the floodplain. Hibou watching Egypt raise its script. By the river where all Egypts store their lightning; underneath the pearly rose of all built things?

To Klang, now made of iron. Made with plates of beaten cladding, stovepipes screwed together weirdly. Now strong again with stories' blood, now silent as the voices' batcloud deserts him on the shore?

And to the third who keeps his station in between them. Who though they never see him, never will, is always exactly at their middle point. Who's the reason they can talk but never talks to them. Who compiles a dictionary because old moss is knitted on the boulder and the boulder sinks slow knit into the banks?

How many came? Strophe, antistrophe, a voice's engine in the lofts?

You won't be hearing from me again.

Klang.

Iron lids to face the iron coast.

Saw him turning toward the rocks. The dragon dormant in the shorepile. Scales' soft mica shed and in its place a work of iron leaves. Tree come forward in the rock skin. Tree, come out and show us where you branch. Show us where the iron petals out with trunk to guide it. Saw him turn to shore's lashed metal, iron crowded from the boulders, light of fogwrapped sun to draw each petal from the last. Sun a globe of smoke behind the cotton.

Above, mist moved too fast. Like sped up film. Mist that meant the world still turns; that nothing in its circuit fell when men fell by the gates. City ground to clink of spearpoints, city shucked to boundary stones that catch the pilgrim fire, city now a ruined strip. So that the gate stands up from nothing, giving onto nothing. So that wall becomes the ruin of a wall. The nameless scrap of brickslope in a heap of endings.

Here we have not kept the panther out.

Here we haven't put a chainlock on the fruit.

Here we haven't bundled weapons, kept straight swords from cracking on the curved ones.

Here the panthers swats a foreleg at the brick, and one more twist of mortar has brief flight.

Saw him bring all this to mind. The lids now gone full iron. The face's wrack, the etched-in grooves of salt, fill out gunmetal. Grey reflective coral in his hair. Coral pink to grace his falling chin. Not reflective. Not exactly sun that's given back in sunshape, in a scarecrow length of willows. But sun become the music in the coral. Sun, grey sun, sun pearled and chewed down pink. The high harmonic of the coral's pipe; the sharpened ice-note when a wave has shivered down that pipe but catches on some horn and shivers up. The reef within the frond-wall. The old stone god asleep inside the seaweed.

Saw him flinch beneath the panther. That he'd seen it and had known the step it followed; that he'd heard the lung-deep growl and had hunkered with its fear. That he saw the ship tied down to seafloor with a flood of rippling vines. That he saw the tendrilled grape burst out along the salt-cracked oars. That he saw live rootcrop coil up through the hold and plant his decks. When one island was a knife and the other was a cave of bitter teeth.

He heard the salt pool crackle in the bilge. Looked over as its surface broke with grapeflesh.

He heard the copper groaning in the mast and watched its ragged grain produce a tiger. Heard the spatter-slap of woodchips hit his deck and watched the rotted wood fall off, revealing inner plant of sculpted bronze.

He felt sharp heather panting in the air.

He felt the pewter reeds within wind's clang.

And now stood on the coast where dragon left its backbone. And now closed eyes against the seaborne wind. Let wind's gold salt set scales upon his face. The brace of coloured sand that ocean's scratch then heated into glass. He wasn't cased. Not put in envelope, not bound by shell. The iron of the shore called up an iron from his blood. Metal coast drew toward the drink of metalled veins. A hundred years of seabreath left deposit on his lung, and ocean now no more deposited: now the bridge to build. Enough outside his inside that the metal, sand, and salt could touch their palms. Erect an ocean tower through his soles, now cockle-gripped.

Saw him as a bright arm of the sea. A moving claw.

Saw all shore behind his motion and all plant turn glass to meet him.

Secret glass that he, as ocean's agent, brought to sight.

And still –

In the stone of seeing deafness, in audition of blind water –

Neither blind nor deaf, but looking so if you weren't the sea –

And still to all his stone and all his iron –

How many voices through the blackwrapped air?

How many sable tongues to beat on batwings through the hurricane? Still the liquor of the voice. Still the glass-shaped fire from tooth-shaped air. Wet bulbs rattle in the far throat; rough weeds lapping in the near. Still he heard the voice of moving pebbles. Still the tunnel gullet full of seeds. And every soil a residue on jagged planes of throat; and every mix of loam a stain from words held back too long, or said too loud, or wasted on a misdirected song. Throat's facets rich with blackblood soil. The dry rill plucked to wetness.

Saw him there with fisher-birds to hunt the voices for him. Condor, heron, and flamingo. Pelican and duck. A smelted crag of iron with a rising bird-tornado for his home. Saw kingfishers rip the quick voice from the fraying threads of sky. Saw the voices show their silver like bright trout between the breezes. Birds to down the song and lay it at his iron-husked feet.

Song dropped limp from seasquall when the condor's howl had felled it.

A pile of silver diamonds set before him.

And he's still shut-eyed iron by the rocks.

So I went to him and heard the pulse still moving. Heard the veins shut hard around no blood; heard the heart's thin chambers work to pump their filed steel dust. And knew that I had known this sound before. Before even I was me. Before there was a chance for me to hear, and hearing was a passage through the lymph. When hearing was a pocket curled in seeds and every seed was waiting. Knew it. Knew it.

I held up the bowl of warm new blood.

I poured it in the small spout of his mouth.

Saw blood touch iron where the excess spilled.

And leaned again to listen; and heard his veins reopen. Heard big arteries go sighing like the air loosed from balloons. Heard the heart's thick flutter, then the rhythm start again. The frame of rhythm's jade that holds a net for every other song. His eyes, still iron, opened. He said: "Stand back a bit."

He picked the first bright voice, still living, from the pile. He said:

"And then ..."

Hibou.

Sat on the hillside. Felt salt of stars, mosaic where his feet had been. The stars' dark magnet planted in the image of his sole: here the frozen curve that keeps them coursing. Here the forking root, the milky snake that plants them with a snap of fangs. Here rip of blastlight out of fabric billows. New snakes born.

Not egg that breaks its hinges in a knot of coloured dust, though that is a real kind of birth. Not live-birth either, snake uncoiled from old snake's inner maze. But the birth condensed in seconds. Where was only black in planes. Where was only hollow ice that held as crystal bone, from time-before to time-completed. Now comes the crack across all stargap: blink of hidden eye that pours out rigid light when it's been lidded. The lash-rub downs a fissured clap of steel. Every magnet turned toward blinking space. Toward blinking time, in the Egyptian field – a chain of oceans out there, where time and space press palm to palm to palm. Magnets turn.

Turn to make a sundial colony. Old machinery whose engine eats the day. Gear made for one turning and one only: when the flood has found this land. When the closest star, the Dog, the Ox, the Viper, finally slits Egypt with its heat. A day and night of sky full up with terrors of the sun. One sun too big for seeing. Skin in boils and chaps, sight gone narrow, black stone like glass become a well that sounds the sky. All old wells dry. The new well, drink of obelisks, pushed up from Earth that only used to gather water down. Beneath the nightmare orange with nightcloth hidden near its ribbons, near its flares. And everyone will look around at wells that stand up, at night that folds and falls behind a wrong and endless day.

And everyone will say: Now we're underground. When the water's hard and stands erect; when sun's a pressing core and every night we dream of digging; when we would dig toward water's sphere. When we would scrape the soil for tuber eyes. Potato's tendril shocked from sheath of dust. When we would climb them up into the dirt, would pierce the canopy called farmland. When we see plants, see any plant, and hope they're ended roots buried in the air – the feet of hanging trees that, if we pull ourselves along their bark, lead us to a dome of water.

When men are made of two portions: what outlasts the day and what the day has claimed. Not just the organ rusting, eye gone some inch more veiled. Not just the stomach acid-bit where once was oily pink, the elbow creak where bone-ash falls in filings, the finger slower bent and slowly straightened. Not just the mouth that spits dry ghosts. That once was singly dry and now has fifty ways to be unwetted. Nor just the hair that worries at the crown; nor just the breast that sinks back toward its heart, to lend more muscle to the only muscle living.

Not just these, though these persist. But also half a year of skin now shed in half an hour; also summer brownness moulted while the winter's meant to sleep. But also eye more milky than a day's milk should provide. Also bone more hollow than it was last night at sleeping – bone turned to weaker sponge, with pores more open, greedy for the final sun. Children tired. Children not able to answer questions. Men not able to answer questions. Women who can't tell you where they've been, who meet the question with a slackened face. Muscle's belt worn out and giving no more tension. Women breaking awful dams when questions lead them there. Stone walls inside them leaking out a juice that pools at death. A fluid, black to purple, that should only fruit in them once: from the dying plant. From broad-leafed night, when women's glide has lasted out the falling afternoon, and ivy death has wound around their fibres. Ivy death entwined with rusty columns in their legs.

The iron rail where iron opens blind eye through its paint.

The gold-dust stone fermented into red.

The calculating cone, nailed up to let a sunstreak pass on the longest day of the year. Now howling stopless vision till it pits the field to rags.

Until: between the furrowed bronze, people moving one direction all, as one, stop moving. Lie down slowly. Not collapse like time has built in them. A slow unlocking. Socket dry and open, bone now bowed against resistance of no tendon. A lying-down with hands prepared to meet the copper dirt. Hands along the face, to guard it from the bronze's blooming spike. Feet turned up and knees first touching soil. This is the last moment.

Other moments follow on, but the wakeless seed is pushed deep into them. Not yet sleep, though sleep may come. Just the end of waking. While a sculptured belt of fire, fire holding plastic form across two times' collision, breathes into the people's dry-planed air.

Egypt gone still. Egypt made of shucked breath on shucked breath.

The river full of fishes' empty husks.

The storehouse full of sheaves that wheat has left, and of the empty wheat's brass rattle.

Will this happen only once?

Sat on the hillside, and reflected that it might not. Reflected that Egypt may have been planted by that burning. Had its soil turned twice, or several hundred times, when laddered star condensed its sweat into a powder.

Sat on the hillside and reflected that it might happen only once, but that it would be unwise to think so.

And so raised the needle. The needle one mile high, with eye to narrow down the blast of coming suns. Sat in the eye-crook. Felt two rays, from two ends of the world, conspiring on our backs. Combined to form new focus: cone that sizzled off the birth-dirt where our city was to rise. Sunheat clear against the dry burn of our days, invisible when night worms through the bracken's pores and nudges water toward the lizard. But on our backs. Felt, not seen. And feeling eyes were open to the rivers in the sky, to the feather-fall of heat without a shape. To the scratch and nod and breath-damp of a beast without dimension.

Over Earth's right curve, the sun is heated cloud-filings, steam that turns and turns until the east is born and steamdisk hums to move the chain of hours. They clank beneath the ground. So slow that you'll just hear them as the back-buzz of your life. The field of sound that carves all other music. Earworld full of plaster that the flies, the flood, the gun will etch on hearing. But they make a sound. We reflected that the hours make a sound; that it's no use to build a city and pretend that they don't. Reflected that the city rumbles under with the hours' drone. That cities come before were planned to ignore time's wire in turning, steady turning sound of time's steel string. That this city, if it could, should bite its taproot into time's foundation. So that when the crumbling comes, we'll recognize its harmony. We or those who take the city next. So that when the lime-crack freezes through the lime, we'll know to live in falling blocks. In cinders. Pipes. Doorways stood in front of nothing, doors that open to a wilderness.

Over Earth's left curve, the sun is night's last dream. Dream of glows that snaps the night awake. That crowds an evil fog around the day night spends in hell. Pomegranate glass with grainy fluid in its beakers. Pomegranate emptied of twelve seeds. A few less or more per day, according to the night-thirst, to the count of water razed off the moon while it was dreaming live. According to the night-thirst. Want of cold and sweet that hangs back in your throat. A metal pan to twist inside your swallow-chamber. Letting metal runoff breed within the fall of cold and sweet; keeping metal thirst between your sating. Reflected that all other cities run on thirst, as ours will run, but lie about their engine. That they run on crowding people from one drink to another. That they are piles of promised drink and take their shape from what drinks shouldn't rub another. Here the granite water/there the gold. Here the bloody water/there the oily.

Reflected that the city's several drinks are proof that none of them will work. That city-people have probably known this, but that they've got to pretend they don't. That the mother's drink is fever and the wife's is shiftless metal, and someone knows that thirst is lightning in between them. Or the father's milk of mercury, the husband's runoff from a mound of funeral soil. Earth a rolling tumour where the crypt is packed with sand. Stitched to half a roll; sewn before the cringe that would expel it.

And so raised the needle. Drew the first night's writing from the reeds and reed-marked dust. From whatever marked our sight so far below: the crow-thick corpse, the pyramid of fruit, the phosphorescent snake. Oranges piled across our little world from piles of skulls. Each the bone-scry globe for a different divining. When the needle hangs from cities' underside, people rub the oranges and growl wildness. People slit the skulls and gorge on subtle juice. Every night the needle shifts its hanging. Scrapes a luminous smear from higher suns and then reports them to the lower. Draws a patch of inner suns' thin oil to fertilize the high suns' furrow. It has happened every day forever.

Reflected that it has happened every day forever.

That no one sees the fruit of empty skulls. That we see the track of dust, the little cataract that grooves their yellow bone; the place of eyes gone jagged and the place where teeth corrupt. But not the fruit or the sweet water. And still we've all drunk it, eaten it, every

15

day forever. Still whatever music haunts that fruit could herd us off in droves if anyone had learned to play it. Still the bone-flute skirts its edge, catches song of skull-fruit when the note is overblown and rasps the mouthpiece as it rasps the evening's gaps. But never quite and never all the way. A touch. A groan. A scrape.

The fingernail over drumhead when they're trying to play with palms. The desert language in its hiss. Called "a mistake."

The whorl's pad down the string when one note dies too soon. Too long before the rising of its daughter. A shaft punched through eight dynasties of Earth. On one side, first note green with age's jade. Propped up between two columns. Come more and more to take the grain of marble. Skin drunk under by the sheen of stone that guards it. On the shaft's other side, daughter-note whose seafoam drills up through the roof of hell. Amid a range of quivering waves made from the flesh of grapes. Grape-meat pressing all the light to purple grey. Daughter-note with honey that she harvests from the rims of clamshells; daughter-note with algae-nested pearls to hang around her; daughter-note with seaweed hair, inside a vaulted god. Body of the god plumed out with ribs to keep our daughter from a scalding rain.

But between them, that shaft. Pit injected through eight dynasties of Earth, we have reflected. And in it, toss of bones from one wall to another. Canvas pocked with falls of fallen sparks. Holy rock – but shadow eats the glint, so we can't quarry. In the shaft, at bottom or in a gallery on the side, giants of every missing age. Now turned to clay. But still alive. And fermenting, on their shoulders, a weather so black that it glows against the blackness.

3rd.

The monoliths rose silver from his shoulders. And the wind sheared rain from waxy rattling leaves. But these were in two different spheres. The second: bowl of night. Where cloud-walk rumbled heavy on the dome. Where lower ocean stilled and gathered atoms for its statues; where the higher ocean wore a mask of trouble. Showed within an hour the roll of tensile darkness that would see a city rise, a city fall. And the first: *one time that he went down.* Began the song with that.

And then went down.

Now silver columns. Obelisks and spheres. That Egypt come to ripeness, then far past. He dove through layers of concrete. City's substance wet to bear his search. Through borderlands marked out inside the soil. Through brace of hollow reeds between two girders of a bridge. Cross-section of cement and ailing iron. Now a wind to sing the coming of their rust. He dove but felt that he was standing still. A frozen bolt in blue protection while an Egypt rose around him. Needle pyramids now puncturing the low-slung day. Finally put off the tense circuit, highway dragonflying dead loops by the towers.

Finally the god whose mass is arms. Whose face is armpatch, fingers for his eyes. The god who hears by grasping sound and pumping it as leaden blood is pushed through heart. Who sees by fingering the sight. Whose lifetime squeezes sluggish bile from liver of clasped hands; who presses out the lymph from vein's collapse. The city is a grove of vessels. Crypt of empty pipes that wait for him to gain the ground and milk them out. This Egypt wants to spread its mottled cream in gouts unpierced by rain. But the god has been a while in getting to it.

Now he goes down by that god's encrusted house. A sapphire hole grown out with crystal teeth. In perfect image of the Egypt's towers above. When crystal finger punches through the roof of hell to crop out god-cave, then this Egypt raises one more spine of steel. The tired god has kept apace. He waits for when the ebony falls dead. For when no marble winds through fertile mud. And then the period of study. Years of feeling out the building's thrust. To know the mothballed birds gone silent in its siding. Know the lion that protects it and the termites who erect its hanging double.

Study Egypt's underside where every pyramid has root. The brain that made men want to build them holds their shape. Sometimes reflects a damage to the structure, sometimes not.

Here's a brain whose upper body lost five floors to plane-crash. Those floors are gone from sculpted root. But up above the hole is jagged iron and calligraphies of jet fuel. Underneath, anemones sprout glowing from the wound.

Goes down where all the gods of dirt make houses. Past sheet metal hallways where the arrow planes the air with killing whisper. Past the mossy throne whose woman is away. Past faded boy who kneels by water's edge, his face locked into bright red vines that crawled out of the lake. Past pale and crosseyed men that pale god nurses at his temples. Trickled hornmilk from the forehead. In anger they burst temple-flesh and tip themselves with gold. In sadness, now, they drip a cloudy juice. Past woman burned alive who wanted to be burned, now charred adornment for the throne of one who killed her. Past the void where ringing rooms once stood whose ringing carves the earscape. Past it all.

Past ruined Egypt. Ruin's belly growing big.

Past every city's underside and then the cities hid in death. The ones whose metal softens now to infiltrate new roots. Who drip the brass like butter till it licks a light-bound vine.

Went down first through the lake. Hard water rigid with its chrome. Blue poison flakes. Try not to breathe. Men or men's duration left a staircase etched in stiffened moss. Stare straight ahead while royal venom closes on your eyes. Don't stray. Or if you do, content yourself to live in sea-fast cities. Lake was once a pregnant pit. Then flood that froze its pregnancy. That wrote upon the child and turned its gummy coat to talisman. Not worse than being born. We think. No better. Writing comes from here.

He writes, we've learned, by sucking mummy fluids from this statue of a child.

Then once the lake's low hatch has given way: the rivers. Cross them with a migraine step. Blood-red leached to orange and then weak pink. His cagework veins are clogged with calcium. The moonfields of his brain give crop of silver coins. Cross this river: hear a clicking stop whose sound you've never noticed. Now will know it's always there. The looms on reddish hillsides stop their song. No more a night cooled with quick stitches. No more cloudplates married by the twine. Night from now will sag and stretch. Unravel.

And in answer, all the bubbling tree that wraps around his skeleton will push away. Blood-hose curled around the elbow squirms to scrape the skin. Blood-branch cuts through gel inside the eye and puts sick garland on his pupil. Part of why live men don't cross these rivers. Man is ivy stitched to ivy. Man's one weave of tendrils folded on another. Bloodtree glued to bonetree. And this river kneads a softness through their glue. The bronze between its water-ply gives off a loosened steam. A swarm of worms that chew the muscle.

When a man has been here long enough, his map of veins sits one place and his bonescript lies another. Certain gods can weave them back again. Put naming-song to places and the flavour to the name. But it's uncommon. Having passed the final river, man is humbled out of carrying his own. Having seen the flood's first writing, man is scared of all the hieroglyphs that once infested him.

¶

Rook. The bird hex. Forms in middle air. Highest reaches of the lowest sky. Region of the plane crash and the burning engine's halo. Region where the pyramid resolves. Fear diamonds at that altitude. The jackal's eye refracting pinkish beams. Mathematics' birth. A cone held pregnant in the sunray sweep; now fathomed out, unstuck from all the sunharp. One gold strand forgets the loom. Then focused on fear's crystal, made to shock the sand with straight-armed glyphs. Still waiting for the fly-pressed stone.

The brick condensed from goldfly and the bugs in trumpets' breathing. Air's column scuttles past the mouthpiece. Then the room incarnate born around it. Boxy edge means room small as a box. The unripe ghost before sound's echo. Phantom comes too early, gives no haunting. Just a cardboard lip hung from the note. But the big outspread of reverb means that player plays near caveroof. Means that underground a cataract has split the figured stone. New water drilled from granite's pocket gushes over cliffbreak. The baby flood effaces stones with seven Egypts chiselled on their flanks. Soft water. Soft but wrapped around erasers. Scrap away the seven writings. First the shrieking scratch. Then starfish lines. Then column fit with limbs. Then walking man. Then walking man arrayed in symbol; second birth of scratches, changed from man to what he says. Then just the lines. And last the lines we read. Now blasted off by tiny vapours. Start the vicious thing again.

Have moon call up a serpent from the river's bulging plate to bite the mountain into words.

Room. Unit of sound. The mouth and throat that come before all music. When the song is grey and fishlike. Folded dragon powerless in arms. The limp spine pokes through skin like settled oil. Scum leaks the rainbow. Hidden armature of music. Room connects the song – mouth's product – to the *Earth* – a belly bomb. Between a tooth-lisp and an acid comes the room. Between a tongue's red wart of rubies and the lining eaten off, there stands the room. Between a face gone cracked with music and a pouch choked up with bile, the room obtains.

It makes the passageway. Song sticks into elastic shape when it passes stomach's nozzle. Hardly more than mess. A blob with rudiments of skull and chest and digits, but no kite of bones to fill their boneless moulds. Dead sail tacked onto nothing. Above the stomach-lock begins the room, and there song wrestles into shape.

Each rubber songsperm struggles differently around the room's white rings. The gristle hoop kicks out a force like burning. Sends some minerals back to the stomach, where they dream of future songs. Others gain the globule's core and select the note to come. Normally the course of sound through room leaves singing pith with one skin's layer.

That's the skin of all its characters: what architecture blasts out of the sound. Which buildings it demands to be torn down and which it howls to have built in their places. Whether grain will shoot through dirt-sieve red or white or brown with locusts. Whether rice will come in clean and shake off shells of rock-fresh water or will grow as just a maggot husk. Whether song will most attract the string, the pipe, the bull's throat flayed and stretched around the hoop. If people sing it when they rub their own dead or when strangers die untouched by hands. If people sing it all the way through or stop after the basic kernel. If it's safe to sing in cities walled with rock; if only cities shaped by brass can hold it; if every city but the last is laid too weak to bear its shudder, and the last one rises up in augur's dream of its own dying.

There is said to be a song that only Ecbatan can hold. And Ecbatan is said to build itself according to the order of stars' impact with the Earth. Build out its rings to take first fires of Mercury, then all the other planets, till the two suns touch each other since the first time since before time. If this is true, we haven't heard it. But then we wouldn't have.

Sometimes the room is broken. That's the cause of song miswired between untouching planes. The sound that growls through elevator shafts but never finds an ear. The song that edges out of ear-whorl but is never heard. The song imagined and unplayed; the song that's played in open air, with people watching, but refuses to have a body. The song we see as silent ridges crusting on the ocean. And as useless gods with torsos split where stoneflower splays the vine.

Whole cultures have been dedicated to keeping up the room. Entire Egypts have been built as models of the perfect room, and people killed or forced to breed because the room was too full or too empty. Or because its volume was correct, but too alive, unpadded by cadavers. Or the opposite. These Egypts have collapsed, as do they all. The science of the room cuts inexact.

Roost. The long nighthouse. Form of border fence for cities in maturity. What's sleek and matted in the daytime but, when day is stillborn into night, comes out in plumes. Last thing sun observes before it climbs into the ivory barge. Begins to look at roost with calm glass in its eye; but when the look is over, wild claw splits the cornea with fear. Sun reels. Sees highway overpass that dangles tentacles of wire. Falling black bodies hung by wires' hook-ends. Sees the pavement underneath grow amber husks as big as men. And each husk holds a windowlight of falling men's last face. The bodies burn out negatives of sky. Not black themselves but black patch torn from ozone and from smog. The wind spreads watery fingers at their edges. Old small wars for gravity recur.

The sun sees overpass let down a frozen mobile made of fallers. The sun sees little saplings with their branches ripped away but with their tenant birds stitched onto the evening. Constellation of orange beaks around the trunk's frail inching sap. The sun sees chicken's eye too full of too-large moon. The sun sees chickens scrambling in a dirt field while the moon's curve presses down. The sun sees shattered people dragged off highway by a towhook in their gills. The sun sees Border dance like centipede and Border's landfill cough up white new women. The filigree of pearl from towering rust. The band of meat alive between dead walls.

All of which to loose the blood from stubborn solar veins. Now when his white boat goes over day's edge, sun will bleed out easy. No slow lymph-slugs in the pit. Free of clots that block the dead throat full of fresh-dead speaking blood. Several Egypts ended when the sun's stuff ran too thick. The dead can't sleep until all blood has passed through them; but the muscles of its passage have gone slack. They can't work out impurities and bulges. So an Egypt's roofed by nightfire when the dead men hack and gargle. So an Egypt's broken grain beneath cicada-storms when dead men climb from hell. All cities are the pillar-nerve that joins their hell and heaven. And when either place is full of reedy chatter, things go evil. When the high sun won't get murdered and the low one thirsts for air, all houses flatten.

Hell and *heaven* are also names for the sun that forms each place. Geography of cities is the press and mould of one sun bucking seabound and the other slicing clouds. Thus all mountains, buildings, people, pets. The growth of pod-faced gods from silent water. Silver fur that moonblast turns to chrome; apples sheathed in gold to loose the spider on our teeth.

The moon is conduit between them. But the *river* is its own hot trench of gods. Does not obey the other bodies and can sometimes own the moon. Thus dreams and writing. Thus the music that works free of time's bent hinge and plants a copper river-snake in earholes. Thus the shellfish that patrol our brains' two sides and sometimes tear from skullmeat, learn to totter on their own. Neither sun can do a thing about it. In their own domains, the upper one is tall and pale and sickly. Shrinks away from his own dogs. Bites underlip at night's new phosphor. And the lower one's a brainmass. Has no feature to display what it might think. Or if it thinks, or if it's been alerted to its hell. It collaborates with river on the city's squalling birth. The upper sun suspects it.

Root. The basic god. Sometimes honoured as the first. Which reference is dangerous and risks the older angers. Crab and damaged dragon. Seaweed grown through statue's pores. The rose's nailgun twined through seawall and the rattle of thonged bones. But the root, if not quite first, is basic. Form of river's low conspiracy with hell sun. Form of tiger through the singing shafts of cane. Form of stripe scorched in the fur when old cat leaned against a cage of bamboo pipes.

We're afraid to say too much about the root. We know the river lets out words and rips them back; we know the river has an agent in our tongues and might get angry if we wrongly sing the root. River makes the flat word disappear across all cities, then kindles it beneath the citadel's weak foot. We're afraid also because the root is in all saying. Not the same root but the rootwork. When a word comes sideways out of circled mouths, the root has nudged it. When a word we meant to whistle shoots out discs that slice the wheat, we've mouthed a root. It knows the growth and death of cities even though we were their builders. It knows how to put the gates and horns and pyramids in sleep's most gleaming corner. How to make us build them. Sometimes built to fall with gem-fire. Sometimes built to be the resonators. Shaft of empty humming when our sons' bones thump against them. (Cf. *room.*)

Though it's impossible to say, the root has probably had more songs addressed to it than any other item. For example:

My beach has filled with needlepoints
Where crabwalk drops the nail, and
You are far away, remember
Nothing of all this.
And:
Cinnamon mimes through the slackened vein.
We're hungry brass. We're bound to horse-neigh
And to be the air where neigh escapes from horse,
To be the pellet of his breath,
And ride
By hanging underneath him.
Couldn't build the city's powder in eight rings.
Couldn't steal that egg from seafloor,
Couldn't dye the spotlit sail and so
Came hard up where an iron worm
Lay crosswise on the shore.
Wish Klang had warned us.
But his flesh is full of iron's knead
And probably connects them in a fraud.
Cannot damn Klang. This is his city.

Hibou.

We have seen the old stone gods consumed by solar fire.

Fire-lick mounting basalt, slate, obsidian. Fire's wet tongue along the less black veins in blackness. One sort of god's blood. In the rocks, called porphyry. The frozen salt, the river's sugared stillness, and the sleek bronze powder seeping in between them. Whispered laugh of alloy: metal mixed to other metal's gesture. Brass arms round the arms of nickel and their marriage leaves stained continents to patch the wall of curving glass. Silver divots in the bronze-bright face. Nickel drops the ingot shape into a cymbal's speaking. The click along its slope is talking brass; but the feathered fade, the fade that speaks and then doesn't speak – in it, nickel's ghost reposes. Lies back, sits up, lies back.

The cymbal-fade that draws out air's dim pulp. Hum planed to planes that move my skull. Cymbal wash around them in a circle, so that scraps of my head's flesh resound, then quiet, then resound again. One buzz for the temple's stretch. Just below the pitch of hearing. One buzz for the back teeth and the shards they drop at night, the clattered hidden works that forks and spoons pronounce on them. One buzz for the under-eye. Pulled down in granites toward the nose. Long cliff's fall wanting to be longer. What my face wants by itself. What it would still want were it no one's face, or no more mine. A lash of ragged leather in a landfill. Teeth to button up invaders' coats. Still the cupped eye-meat would strain into its falling; still the nose-knot, triple broken, with all weather gasping from its pores.

Undropped rain is hardness, swelling, pain. Rain that drops is tender. Sore. Whine of block-shaped air that's found a pinhole valve.

And there is a sun that scrapes the side of brain's cocoon. Sun deeper than its light, or higher, on the frequency of knives. And in that sun, I feel a lifeless breeding. I feel wasp instinct fold stone to its purpose. Wasp house built from chatter of mathematics in the eyes. The burning song with burning sides, a sound of tunnels closing; the burning maths whose numbers mean four rooms of cold grey mud. The wasp egg in my skull has wrought its engine. The stingers strain to crawl out of my husk.

We have seen the old stone gods consumed by solar fire.

The sun that ate them had a fold. A reddened middle belt. It disappeared when old god disappeared. Ten grains of molten rock in melted seas. His magnet now dispersed. Left in what things he touched, what songs were found to draw him from the amber. Say *heather, canebrake, bracken clutch*. Say *gourd* and *fruit* and *wire*.

Say *white bull* and let its white sides bleed on circled stone.

Bull passes with a red square inked upon its side. A line across the square's length. Was the symbol for the folded sun that ate our worship-rocks. Painted on the bull to recollect the sun's now-scattered horns. Horn rattled in the memory, in purple depths of surf, in children's speech. *Don't let us forget.* The sun has horns. As many as the days before its fold; as many as days after. And more. The sun can gore you on its dash and walk out of the fields with bleeding things still hung there.

So paint the emblem on a bull. If you kill it, skin it, drain its blood to mix ghosts' talking drink, this is no victory. The sun dies every night. As may the bull. Tomorrow it will rise, a rank of white bulls to attend it.

If you have defence, it's narrowed diaphragm. It's fragile lens. The yearless eye with focus where the god moves with the root.

Now Apeliota winds. And now day's dome is trimmed with ozone burn. Now Apeliota barrels circling winds through canebrake. Now the bracken talks with sound of rain, with alphabet of rain through lisping leaves.

Because now Zephyr bellows in the Earth. He goes under. Hills and flatland shiver with his moving. Earth beat down by flickered figures in a night between the night and day. A night that came as hollow, as a space where no more sun could open out and no more moonray give its milk to skin. This night slit the round of rolling spheres. Found the fabric's grid and crawled between. I don't know how. I've only seen the aftermath. Seen where this night clattered on the dust and raised its cymbal. Where this night's broken wood was downed with rattles and its sky held back the moon. Denied the sun.

Sun and moon and starry wheels locked down behind the sheet-black.

Prelude to Apeliota's winding.

The long line arched behind the sphere. Magnetic cone with sphere balled in its point, with Venus, Saturn, Mars to whet the tip and everything a traction in its wake. One night came beneath those cones and knew. One night caught the freeze inside the circuit, spun hard sugar from the course. One night broke the tide between gods' circles. Where everything was motion, motion spinning next to spinning, one night saw the stillness in the motion and drew clamour from the silent breath of space.

Not heard from far away. Not heard even from the middle distance. Only when I drew too close, when I could feel their notice on my arms. Only then I heard. Could hear the slap of rough-lined feet in dust trough. On crest of dirty breaker. On the grass-harp strung to bear this one night's tuning. The ringing chord kept up by feet that tapped. Chord made of knotted bulges, glass planes hitting edgewise, held from shatter by the song. And song likewise a song-knot, clear cold voices falling toward the singer. For a moment pressed against sky's underroof. Clouds of stone-ash billow out their caves in glimpse of lightning. City pressed beneath the granite dome. The sea inverted by position and by substance: above us now and etched from old volcanoes.

City underneath one night's suspension of dead ash.

It can't hold up there for too much longer.

The moment when the red stone hits and Earth is closed – for minute, day, for aeon – in a shell of broken soil.

That's the moment of this hidden night. The only atmosphere that it can breathe; the only moving water that sustains it. Black tide on the shore's black lip, moonglow batted back against the distant web of time. The stars for once look like they really look: nothing. No shaft of time. No time-cone through the black to summon up dead chambers. Dead furnace holding onto dying light. Reactor where the engine has gone out, the sulphur has refused the platinum, the gold disperses wire and won't cohere.

The gold will not cohere.

So that, on the night I saw, my head was punched with starholes for each star excised above. Felt an inner skin between my brain and skull go ragged with light's pinpoint. A membrane that had slept till then. Brittle envelope without a purpose on the rest of days and dormant where the rest of nights massage it. But held back on the skull's blunt curve for this one night. Tuned to this one beat of terror-dancing. Or to all its crosswise beat, enclosed around the clash of chatters as around my brain. My sparking-basin.

One wrapping-sheet of vegetable protection: now cropped out with whistling holes to hoard defunctive light.

Felt that other men had felt this.

Felt dead women stepping forward from my frame.

Dead children's faces jolting from my sides.

Called up like a funnel in the water. Like a bolt that leaves its writing through the tree. Signature on all receiving things. Not the thing, but what repeating nights have written on it. Felt that all the dead have felt this. That dead women know its growing in their wombs, dead men its shape inside their brow-knots. Felt that being dead is partly being this: a signature. A script that one sharp night can draw up from the forest's marble.

Trees now dim white stone, grass now dim white stone, dancers locked in stone reserve of dancing. Blotches, veins upon them coloured dim rose. Zephyr, in the ground, pushed up the stone that sleeps in plant-soil. Apeliota thrummed it and I heard the dead returning. What shows up when the field has been shoved down; what detail rises off the low relief.

Felt the dead make up a walled resistance. Felt the Earth's gold centre, where the wind and vine and sun are brewed, throwing out all weather's ocean. And the dead composed a barrier. A coral shelf that focused rampant seas. Without them, only water's wrack forever. Just the flood. Without the dead, the flood. But with them, with their coiled stone mass, a shape from surging fluid. An ocean with a cup. A rolling basin. With the dead, a flood in borders. Shipwreck roots to trail their bone-fed lilies to the surface. With the dead, a lotus from the marble and a white rose on the night. With the dead, an ancient music with one night for shield and boundary-stone.

The night that I'll return to every time I hear the dead.

Open out of other night's loose seam.

The night that builds brass Egypt.

Egypt sleeps in host beneath the hill, between the dust. Egypt hides between the golden brick. Egypt is the river and the river's face beneath it. And one night, borne up by Zephyr, with Apeliota's pluck, I heard the mass of coral dead become a focus. Music formed inside their dome. Day's dome, night's dome missing for an hour. And all the dead as Egypt's future people. The gust that makes the seaweed god stand up out of the sea.

3ʳᵈ.

They dredge it from the belly of a snake. Long belly walls contracted on a static: trace the clashing ray through mud and wood and blackspace. Once a music. Now a music still, but walled by different measure. Static's lift of ridge to grind on ridge and make the snowfall; static's mane of pricks from empty channel. There is no empty channel. Even when the name of bands was undiscovered, when the warm receiving meat had not yet woven grid of voices. When there weren't any channels by the name. Still none of them went empty. Always static made of sun's black hair in daytime. Always static nights shook off the snorting star. The cloud of star's breath heat-lost, alkaline, on sea that's only surface. Before the dredging led to dredging led to city. And the city led to city led to voice that had to be where it wasn't; led to dead voice strong with copper wiring's blood.

Led to where the dead have always lapped from vein's abrupt new mouth. The frigid dirt black-spattering on the hoe. The arm put down to lend its elbow's map for sounding pits. And out of distant house, a hulk with mist-wiped face, come droves of dead like fog-stunned sheep. A shamble speaking fur and horns they've sprouted since the world. Out of the house's shifting plates. The metal skin that changes softness so you never guess the lymph. Where kidney lends its shellmeat to the yearly aching worm. Where stomach vaults the acid's roil and heart is battered by its function. Out of the house of lowered eyelids where no eye can spin strange light. Where light derives no matter, so the eye's rind fills with lead.

A band of heavy salt in crease of eyelid leather. A band of static, coiling slow with two-tone flares, unfurls from slit gut of the snake.

They knew where day-downed sun had frozen. Knew the kink in molepath and the broken fork of water's thousand arrows. They knew where lizard doesn't sun because the heat won't take. Won't break the rust-darned skin. They knew where puddle ramifies to limb, pregnant with the soundless bulge, and needle seizes on its helicopter string. Wind up. Unwind. Wind up again. But here the winding cracks. A rest from always winding everywhere. The day, the year, the fat-stained flow in failing human rivers. Sides worn down to listless sag. Gone slack with passing tumours; gone to ribbons underneath the grate and scrape of crystal salts.

Here a measure blooms like cancer in that winding. Mottled blackspot on the lung of weavers' breeze. But still a weave and wind for eye scaled up to earthtime. And beyond that, planets crash. A pinhole's violent green borne up from night to night. First shock in skywall; then a spot; then sheathed green coin, an essence algae pressed from gold; and finally a third of sky, a half, a more-than-half. At last the sky replaced and foreign hollows on the screaming. Voice clicks back to swift delay of planet's face. Unknown before. The gasp of tongue-jabs when another planet's crater has received them. At last the end.

At last a burning iris flowers through the lake of cold.

And still, there will be eyes to call this weaving. You've called it that just now. By thinking of the name.

Man hears a drone of vowels when another man splits iron from its hillside. Man considers that this may be corpse of god. Man wonders at the god-corpse shattered, melted, welded back to line the city. Man considers that the city built would be new meat on god, would speed his tent of bones through new white lime and give him hunger. Man's afraid of hungry god. Man thinks of split god secret in the fibreglass, between the slabs of pounded dust, a god-cage spanning god-ribbed air from feet to soundless ceiling. Man is hungry but afraid. Man checks his feeling. Man is now afraid but hungry. Join the wilted stem to one who wilts unfinished; pleach the arbour where it's nearly dead to vine where death looms farther. Man's afraid to build a city where the god has seed of wrath and limns bone-pivot inside everything. It seems unwise. But less unwise than no new city. Less unwise than drying out beneath a sun days wreathe in dust, than letting dust-scythe slide a skin from him by hours until the last hour finds no skin to cure his brain.

And so the god is disassembled. Whittled down to standing rods. They hold erect his alien marriage. Forced to join with strange new gods no younger than he is, but later come to iron's coast. Strange god of ground-down shells, the waste trail of the worm. Strange god of stolen furnace, copper blast of inner sun now transferred to the day. Strange god with hammer's face and body like a stalk. The old one living deep within them. Both the one that's driven deep and one that finds a prison. Both the icepick and the cell of cold that doesn't break. Now married in the bone with strangers' marrow. So the city.

But old god can hide his blood. We're greedy for it, need it obvious. We suck it from the cradle. And when dead we ask a cradle's grace to rock on frozen mud. We ask the cradle bars to line a ragged pit and red remembered blood to be our speaking drink. It's seen and heard. It's penny savour dowsed by frostbit tongues. The old man of the iron bleeds in secret. Can put iron veil's refinement on his juice. Can blast a rarefaction through the bones of iron like the bones that now are rib to city's chamber. He can hide it through all hiding. He can put a plaguey river where the live one should've been and loose his blood in red-horned locusts on the night that dared to dig.

The old man of the iron swarms with shrill cicada blast. We call him dry. We call him plaguestricken, felled by shot disease that brought down buffalo. But in the bug's dry horn, an iron blood is singing for the day when cities split.

Hibou.

The grinding in the metal box is passed. And with it, gear and fan will pass unnumbered. Fanblade slid across the bright globes of the night and giving shadow-milk to things' unshadowed darkness. Seen. And known, from seeing, back inside a narrowed focus. Cut by long-piled time into a glasseyed circle. One portal through the loam. Across it pass the compound ghosts. But in a different passing than the clamour passed from this night's metal boxes. Ghost of vinestalk, arching bone, and wreath of metal berries. Ghost of eye in constant quickness, downed from any angle with the fine jade threads of flashing.

As when they yelled out for more blood and I had to find it.

As when the compound ghosts had lapped last bloodstreak from my iron bowl. And they would talk no more without the soft goats' blood to fuel their speech.

Klang.

The diamond is your hair, barred from the wind. And your hair was diamond clamour when the pavements rained around us. Rustled slip of plane on plane. Facet wriggles from the facet's glassy sheen. A race of edges clattered in the day. Half down below its dawning, headed under dawn to come. The air was grey and puffed with rainy pockets; and your hair made diamond slices through its heaving. All air around us drawn by foggy breath. A canopy gone slack at sides to drip and harden as a cave that clipped our seeing.

A couple of your hair's loose strands made surveillance, red, wire-bright. Feelers of a diamond. Diamond listing through the coral scurf, diamond softly landed in blue dirt like powder. Up through five blue miles of rippling glass. Underneath the domelights where the diamonds roll in silence. You can see the conference of their light, the oxidized blade-rattle when one light pulls sharp against another. When one light stares out a shaft that cripples light like halos, windows, portholes. There's a quiet war there. One wins and then the other wins. Time's a row of sutures on that war. Fleshwounds on the face of watered diamond, glassy drink still dribbling from their pale lips.

Dead skin the wounds don't carry off: it flaps around the opening until its white forgets. White dries first, then comes out with a dew not from the other skin. A liquid white that rubs away the skin's own furrowed map. Still hung in tatters from the ending of old husk. But forgotten now. Where it was supposed to be. What thing it was meant to do for skin. And whether yarn on winding posts, dipped down like wavetrough in between the pegs, would lead it back to nestle in that inmost whorl. The pattern broken, mouthing now on sheer blank walls of space. No more feeding from itself. No more gut that feeds the gut with wandering. Now a flap of blanched skin engraved with lines that shock against the world; now plugged into dreaming rows, plugs everysize. The other skin reels and stumbles to crane back and see what skinmaps fasten onto now.

There is a heap of metal Babylon that towers under saffron burn.

There is a furnace that breaks out in faces like a mesh disease. Breaks out in figures and in lips. Just enough grooved dent seared in below the bumps, below the X that fathers X. And when they're looked on with a face, they throw back looking as a mass of faces. Also plugs, also organs, also animals. The rest of you leaned back until it almost fell. It couldn't train its gears to look that high, or train its feet and head together so they'd know the Babylon's one size. That it was all one thing and slouched there as a compound lion. That this whole rank of metal cats, whose height was time, whose stratum-lines were the residue of time's hard seizing, was also one thing altogether.

Faced up to a shaft of iron-yowling jaws, I saw you getting dizzy.

But that was something else. That was in the quiet war of crystals, on a ground beneath the ground, beneath the water. I was going to tell you how it came to us. I was going to say: Look. The crystal carnage throws a milk against the sea's first roof. It doesn't come up all the way to waves. There it would crackle and disperse. The sea would bark a clear mosaic through it, with a sound like wind through beaten canvas. Not even our diamond-dead can hold against the ocean's ancient breaking. But look. Look how it congeals into a skin. Just below the sea-top. In the leaves of ocean's rooftree, where first *shhh* was rasped into the ceiling. Where the sound of boughs against the pounded clay said: *though it's still a room, it's also a box for owls. Though you sleep against the choir of sleeps outside, and the night leaves them unnumbered, still this is a place where sparrows gutter in the corners. Still flamingos watch the grinding pool where wall meets wall and pluck it with impossible legs. Still the leaves creak down like no one's there to read them.*

And if a fire breaks out, it's fire as in the open; and it knows a quick design to marry houses to the night of interrupted dark. It knows a plan that fastens all your living to the living everywhere. And there's no glass or metal sharp enough to shore against the fire's secret planning.

I wanted to tell you that. I was going to. But your hair clanged with red diamonds while more blatant stones cut rain.

Day scorched along its falling line. The tree leaved with two fruits. One a mass of sear, a grove of brittle horses. Stonecrop gold. The neigh has passed their mouths. They utter nothing but the small gold plate where day retreats. Where night leaves its impression. Horses caught in hoof-lift. All wild howling sucked into the wind. Become a fixative: howling wound around their spindle legs, howling stripped of lung-nest to apply glue to the wind. Horse-yowl turned cement. I see where sky's enamel takes the grey translucent sheet. Set pattern of lost neighing. See where skywall's pitted. And on the bruise and crumble, now the thick-neigh border. Gesso lump where horse need was the strongest. Sheet of cracked grey sugarglass that marks the ending edge.

I woke as it shut on the city. The rumble of its mechanism tossed me out of sleep. And now I'm awake to night's beginning; day is chain of frozen suns behind me. Afterimage burned onto the sky. Still silver in the frost and forenoon yellow. But no more heat now. Light of light's reflection. And the bone-ghosts in the face that are unseen beneath its fire now show design. Ghost of rotted porcelain to hold the sun's gaunt cheek. Ghost of seven metals in the mouth. Each tooth the wormshell holding different heaven. Seashell ghost at root of tongue. The mollusc still within me. (The meatbulb, given eyes, becomes the animal.)

Now half a dozen dead-sun photos on the sky. Light only where the torch that left the image still holds place. Setting west, brief flame inside Apeliota. Mating chant to Zephyr so he'll mount the hollow night. Light only where the living sun's orange fluid hasn't settled. Where a sinkhole bears its little slosh. A puddle under girders flecked with last oilpatch of sun.

In construction sites, the train-god still talks heavy; and the sun's last brazen car is brought into their dying water. Construction site. The god's first skeleton. The sleeping god become a prince of death when brickwork moulds his casket. Could be allowed to stay in present shape. To walk on spokes and wiring where the chickens scatter. To put down bevelled foot between the grackle's grunt and shriek. To live with other god shot through his bone-pores. Tremble as the ocean rolls across him. Tremble as the moon picks through his gridwork.

But they won't let him stay that way.

They'll lath a veintree mortar-thick around him. Lock him in the reproductive cycle of cement. Will marry glass and fish, anemone, to suffocate his piping. Give him further pipes that he can't use. Brass and lead and copper. Fill his gut with vents for heat and cool, but the heat and cool of others. Nothing for the god's fierce temperature. Wire-ends sputter in a hollow wall. Wire-ends' quick ratstep at the bottom of an airshaft. Rats pick through oesophagus of alligator clips to find live food or shelter. Delicate among the corpses of the first rat, next rat, last rat. Had to gnaw the sparking juice from wiretip. Had to stand where black coils make an altar. Now a lump of melted fur. Meat-drift under patch of ragged ash.

Or not delicate.

Chewing on the rat-death. Curl of wasted flesh from dark cadavers.

This inside the god's unnumbered shafts. He who stands now where he might have started walking. He whose walk will rest potential in the masonry. Some of us may still be by to see it. With a magnet in the nosebridge that can draw out brick-stopped motion.

As on that day. Every face that day.

Before Egypt had begun. But I felt it stirring the faces' gum. Looked around in blankness of the day. Waiting for the night to put them wild. Can't see a face in daylight. Only see the action there, small action, shift of papers. Only see that something has gone well and something badly. Something unexpected has appeared; another thing awaited and then absent. Complaints of liver, feet. Complaints of numbers. The shield-arm raised into another orbit. Not the shield of night, a focus for the cancer and the dream, but day's white shield that keeps them in their places. The face caught still. No passage over it. What seems to pass is just one curve in ending, so the same curve can begin. I've learned this. There are no faces in the day.

Or if there are, the people whom they mask are silver's agents. Constellation of the night, in gold-touched silver, breathing low behind their eyes. If a person has a real face in the daytime, that person is a chaos-bed of flowers. Any marble city rises from her any point. Any site on her can breed the new steel god. She's alive and dangerous.

She's rabid with the dead and sings their weight.

The density of dead men's coral wall.

The fire-worm always turning in their caves.

If a woman has a face beneath the sun, you'll have to feed her blood. Then she'll do you all the voices. And you'll know what sentence flapped hard in the air. What phrase was bubbled from the lake. What name will focus down the coming night into a ray. Direct that ray across the wastes. Burn in a map for unconstructed city's coloured rings. The city, still asleep beneath the ground, that waits for stellar oil to funnel down into its walls. Each wall one ring; each ring the petrol star that will destroy it.

The face is rare in daytime.

But that day, I turned to see a dead man's face. And turned away and other dead men rose. Dead women there. Live eyes behind starched skin. Live glance beneath the sculpture of dead hair. The people were alive as any people, any day. But they moved that day behind dead people's faces. Bowl of wax that left a dead impression. Faces of the ones who crowded round my boat and cried for blood. Faces of the ones who crawled out of the country when we burned our sheep and bulls. Faces ocean-carved into the oars. Each live person's face erased by dead men's furnace, moulded back with dead men's hands to show the thousand years that chiselled every line.

I looked around that day. I saw.

And I was quiet.

But in my chest-voice, voice that sings from ribs and knows the ribcage words, I was yelling: Now more animals. More blood to wet the dead.

Hibou.

Where were trains, there now are trains. But their rattled shells have passed beneath the arc of different season. The city they were built to etch alluvial, city etched to wind around them, now shifts on different plates.

Where were grain and grain's gold parasite. The second shell whose shudder held another train. Held by thin sheet-metal walls to mime down train's long motion. Train a patterned bending and the air a warp of silky meat between them. Air numbered into strands, pulled against the blacker-pulling train. Where were air-shafts broken with the signal light. Where were knots of aircord dropped and bred in alien fields. Air turned into braids, some thousand locks for every jolted mile. Dropped when train comes to a buckling in the rooftree's tent of oil. Where were trees that prick the sky to take their saps' black tongue. Where were cloud compressed. No more tower and coral piping, but a canvas blacked with oilsmoke, browned with smoke of grass that fall has sucked. Filigreed with silver chaff blown from the silo's curve.

Where was wind that scratched a load of silver from the city's lead-laced paint.

Where were these –

There now are these. But the steam has crumpled out of them. Their edges bubble on the edgeless night. Their walls sprout empty veins. Oxygen-sick artery; the prior blood can't pass. Artery borne up with fatted rust; the old clot, train's old killer, has no map for you. Where were veins tooled in the tin, an awl that whined the chatter-rocks to starbed, now another sound. Another pitch of sky to stick that sound's appearance. Tar of different grasp. Tar not pulled from bonepit and from tigers matted down into the deepest heat.

Not a chain of caverns where dead tiger flows in pitch around his imprint on the grass.

Not a row of galleries, dream-huge and with a Venus-tinted pinhole giving onto other rows. Not the tiger as he knew it. Heather crushed above, a flat spot on the tiger's birthworld. Twined rush bed, fall of honeyed sickles. Not the tiger sunken through the Earth's live belts, come to this place as pith of moving oil.

The old veins' sound. Dry histories of intravenous echo.

Hush of oil, now drained, turns slowly in the empty room. The door that train would rattle off its frame. The glass that train got pregnant with a hive. Wasp-glass live with train's young colony. Bee-glass gives stone honey to the wastes.

The empty room. Dry echo of the empty artery. Only wind in empty rooms. Turned about no centre. Garland on no pole. There to turn until there's no more echo in it. When the clapboard stops its carillon. The windows bear no insect fruit. The roofpeak is no mixing-dome, no place for sounds to seep plane over plane until they bring the rain. Music's rain inside the house. Steel dewbead on the ceiling.

Where were hisses are now echoes. But the echo of a tone that never sounded first; the echo of bell whose strike and lapping gong is quiet in no memory. Where were trains, there now are trains; but they sound the Earth for echoes with no forebear. Catch reflection gleaming off no older song. The echoed soft tornado in the empty house does not obey the older law of spinning. Where were echoes made from prior music's filings, now the echo murmurs something not yet heard.

Speaks the gristly tongue of dark new tendrils born to bite through bright new rock.

The picture-tongue of roots whose echo is their primal iteration. Roots never yet sprouted. For all their time beneath the quarried world. For all their life, an inner sun as hot as memory on their backs. The other sun, in orbit, still a rumour out beyond the iron roof. New echo talks like roots who've never lived except with tigers. Finger-search and groping in the black. Finger-drill among the pitchy tiger ghosts called statue, sea, black gold. Called old god.

And called "old god," the tigers too put foreign echo to your blood. Strange filament along blood-river's chop. A chemical you know is old, beyond remembering, but have never touched or named. All oldness in its smell, its clang, the way it burns beneath your vision. But a smell and sound and star-consequent burn you've never known. Curled around the plant that curls inside you.

A black-grained vine around the rose whose red grain sticks your heart.

Music of stone towers, of living metal –
Injected through the touch of heartrose thorns.

Black dirt dazed with stoneglow. At its centre, drowsy eyelet.
A tunnel's opening. Where shadow-god and vegetation pound.
Where leaf and vine have stalked your eye forever and their stalking
is still new.

Where was city bending to the train, with trainlight in its stem,
there now is pad of cats between dark poles. Shadow-spokes
thrown out by cats in silent stepping. Where was trainlight that
put bending in the city's stalk, released the crooked fluid and the
sugar that made cities nod its way, there now is carlight. And if the
car lights on a cat, two discs of brass or orange or poisoned jade
give back the flash of car's quick passing. The cat lamp only burns
by instants. The diamond now comes forward in the cat when
asphalt growl and harpstruck grass retrieve it. Cat's head full of
diamonds. Drop golden pills, drop ambered moths. But only now
when touched with carlight's glare.

And beneath the roof that roofs nothing –

And between the walls not stretched between their struts, the
walls not winnowed from night's violent tent –

And among the poles that hold a softly groaning chamber, hold
down wind caught by the roof and drag it along mud's mountain
range –

Wring music from the slide of layered night. One ply scratching
on another. All plies taking crook and tooth and crown-edge from
the spine of stiffened mud that arches here as on the last floor of
the sea.

The wind embalmed in ocean makes a bottled sound, a song
closed in a skin, when its sinew rolls along the seabed's bone.

¶

Mouth. Popular mollusc. The mouth will throw you up against a leather seam. It will press you from the inside. A red curled oyster tuned to water thick and white as milk. Blue wisps rip through it. To *travel* sometimes means a climbing down the oyster's hardened branches. Come to a damp and quiet place. While the sky is muscled tarp and every word sets off a heaving. The mouth lives inside you and pretends to be you when you need pretending. It makes blind lunges for the food stuck to your teeth. Though deaf it feels the groundswell of a word. Its underwater heat. Words like magma webbed into the womb of rocks. And when it feels the word come jerking through it, the mouth plays dumb impression of your speaking.

It will talk to other mouths to save you from embarrassment. It will feel the way that air gusts warm and fouled from other people. It will study that sick wind in secret moments. When you're asleep, or dead, or otherwise not thinking of the mouth. In the calm pools of a damp disease like jungle rot, the mouth will reach and sound for proper words. All speaking is the outpour of this research. The mouth imitates to set you soft with imitation's bark. But because the mouth blind and deaf and senseless, speaking is a thick-tongued thing.

Words aloud hunch shaggy in the coat of their own mouth's confusion. Words aloud are glued with too much fur and can't get dry by any fire. Words aloud are broken by the yoke of inner moons. The blue-white moons, the white cream shot with blue that sloshes through a mouth's cool rest. Words aloud can strip the skin from cactuses and drill them dry where should be desert water. Warmish water caked atop a crust of dirt. Mottled with a row of patches, maybe metal, maybe limes. Inside the desert you should – has this ever happened? Inside the desert you should find a drink where metal leaps itself to shine like citrus. Where lime and orange and lemon flash as shields. Where limber trees are heavy with the metal juice in casing. But speaking words aloud will make this hard. Hard up to impossible.

And never speaking would be even harder. People have done it, but they died. So die; or talk the scattered talk, the greasy talk of sliding husks, the big-eyed expert talk. Learn the sour talk for friends, the doleful flannel talk. And let the metal juice break like a bandolier through small dreams. Dreams that walk your eyelids with a pat of gentle feet. Taste the juice by sucking there, where dreaming is a hollow breath, and learn to have forgotten it by morning.

Mouth-breeder. Murderers. People who forgot the mouth that gibbers when they sleep. Or sleeps when they would have it gibbering. People who don't remember where the spit goes after it's been thin and crinkled on the tongue. Who've never thought of silver mines, trellised into nightfire, that roll beside their teeth. The mouth-breeder is violent but at first will seem to be a joke. She (they're not always female, but for the moment let's say *she*) will make you wonder. Her mouth will seem to be connected to its words. When they march across your hearing, you won't take them as a crippled company. You'll forget the moon, the milk, the bitter garment. The herb that dies beneath a grid of wiry fabric; the tree that dies into a rock and hangs a god from rock-bit roots.

Don't forget. Don't forget that. But you will, because the mouth-breeder will force you to. With tiny vises, with a cornsilk laugh. With a jump that shakes between your stomach and your heart. That shoves them out of orbit. Confuses their two drinks, pollinates the empty belt between their different feeding. That's the start of murder. But you won't think so. I know enough to tell you and sometimes even I don't think so. Which is wrong. You're wrong, I'm wrong, the mouth-breeder may be wrong herself. She may not know the scalpels taped along her tongue's red foot. The listening devices stitched beneath her skin. That pose as birthmarks, scars, tattoos. She may not know that tape is dying everywhere inside her, and that in death the tape winds hard around her meat.

Dying tape shed grey in iron drizzle. Iron frost baked brown with brown hard glaze. And falling with a small explosion on her shoulder, ribcage, calf. The tape sheds off at each of her hinges. And each to each white bone, it sears away the sinew and the tendons. Every gluey string inside her snaps like catgut. Magnetic tape replaces it. Her femurs bloom a pair of tape Medusas where they wave below the pelvis. Her knees are whisper sockets with a tape calligraphy curled out of all their angles. Tape slithers in between her small sharp teeth; tape rusts a filigree between the thousand tiny windchimes of her feet. She doesn't know, she doesn't know. You won't. I know now and cough the hymn of killing tape. But soon, soon as tonight or any dark tomorrow, I'll forget and lie and rampage. And when the cure whips burn across us, we'll break like grackles. And we won't understand each other's shrieking, though other people think we sound the same.

Mouth-angel. Out of order because it's not a word yet. It will be. Small mammal like a stretched bat. Hovers in the zone of mouths and picks mosquitoes from their air. Parts the grasshoppers that terrorize your mouthfield so you can walk between them. Sometimes visible beneath big lamps. Sodium engulfs the parking lot with speckled white and angels of mouth turn cursive phrase inside it. If you see one, look at how it's just about to be a word. Look at the ribbon letters arcing from its back. Listen high inside you for a mouth-note, and watch the furry angel slide it softly up the scale. Look up through night's round shutter. The tiny aperture that clicks on nightpeak. And see the saving music dangled from it like the frill-tossed legs of jellyfish; and know the mouth-angel is up there, plucking shadowed looms.

Mow. Unlatch the rank of blades inside your throat and walk them through the waxy grass.

Muck. Where the mouth-angel is witnessed. Sometimes. When said aloud, the sticky −ck clap twines lightning figures on the muck's brown surface. In those moments, any light that finds the muck will take a photo of whatever sleeps beneath it. Every plain of muck rolls back someday; when it does, you can search the riverbed for all those photographs. You can number off the ridgebacked worms that used to marry sheetrock when the muck was in its flowing season.

Mucus. Habitat of the mouth. Too much will let the mouth control your whole head and say its own thick words. Too little dries the mouth into a fossil, and though you'll think you're speaking, really it's just ashy wind that bowls up from your stomach.

Muezzin. Most forked form of electricity. An acrobat who bleeds the sun, who heats that blood to mist, who puts the sunpink fog in cylinders to power his own flight. An acrobat who chimes inside a sunbright cage and taps against the wobbly bars.

Klang.

That's sleepwalking too.

Though your sleep's laid otherwise about you. Not the brainswirled bark along the limb. Not the dulled brown fibre hiding fire's burnish, not the lacquered night that steals space on your eye. One eye feels before the other. Always one with more antennae bristled toward the night. Always one whose iron plates shift open for first daybeam. And then the yellow floodlight through the flooded blue of hell. Not the tortured hell; the hell of fossil caverns. Fossil stars borne down into the squid's twist. Chilled to rock as sleepwalk mounts you with its bark.

The yellow floodlight barely opens through hell-blue, hell where sun goes in his ivory boat. Glancing scythe of yellow on the blue of sun's numbed pulse. Blood no more stretched with red on white. Lymph no more rampant by the membrane. No white fat-knot riddled with the acid.

Brain retreats beneath the sleeping bark.

Spends a night in hive-talk with the bees. Wasp sees wasp-impression on the orchid; wasp lays down its shadow on the brain. Waking with a foreign crease upon your mind. With a gentle dent that sinks your recognition. That's called the dream. Dreams the shade-scratched animals that crawl along your brain when sleep has barked it. Set in shave of marble trees. Just as the sun in dying boat.

And because the dormant vessel under wood –

And because the quiet vein coughs flattened in the sun –

Star.

And star's all-silent wheel. All large. All huge beyond the name and mark of hugeness. Because the empty artery just downed with blood-pause dust: star. As sailor, found my mark by numbering vessels of the sun. When sun-drums clattered dull, stretched out the grid of rope and numbered vessels milklined on the stars. There upon the boat's curved floor. Bark shorn off to keep the bark from fingering my brain. Laid up and looked at ropesquares; looked up where I'd made coral arrows, laid them on the rope. An arrow for the route. Another for the routes that break and branch. Stripped the reef's top hair to make my lines. Cut freezelocks from the waiting god.

Fated, then, to take the coral way.

To take all routes embalmed with coral's valve. No route more straight than pink god's hair had shown it. Every way a chain between the vortex.

Every way a hissing link between the killer pools.

Too late to offer sheepchain, ramchain, chain that sun- and grass-god hide in cows. Too late now. No more replace the snapped-off hair with other twist minced out of other belly. That's the way. Can no more take the way. When god breaks up, you slice a matched part back and keep it safe. Otherwise dead god. And then no use in having coral for the compass: sight would shatter. Vision paled. Except new vision on the god's long corpse. But that means whole new life of careful seeing. And here I am, already on the ocean.

So too late now for boar's intestine garland. Too late for the hanging meat.

Or for the parts that god can bend to match. The two-fold fat where thighbone shows its brand. The white on white of beaten barley. Oatcrop full of sun's bright sweat, turned back to sun in full gut of the ram. Turned back to sun's white death in fold of ram's fat.

Animal is lined with ivory.

Animal is lined with marbled pearl of sun's white dying-bark.

Animal is made from shell sleep-latched around the brain.

And so the sun. Its season. Sweat to death and death lies cooled to dryness. The chamber loud with chemicals gets balled into the barley's golden brain. Then cow-mouth, man-mouth, mouth of god can draw it out. Put sun back in the circulating juice. Now livid blood again, though sun has died. And when I slit the animal to please the throatslit god, I wrench away the sun-held fat again. You see that sleeping always sings the blood. You see that no one sleep can sever all the singing.

Except for that last sleep. When god gets killed: one god, maybe all of them.

Then is long lead quiet in the blood. Then is wave still wave but absent of its metals. Of course to come again.

But then another life at seeing's peak. And that is life too long. When sun stays too much dead for crawling Earth. That means the ashen cloud between our arteries and meat, the shards of stone-cured dog to crack the flow of star. Too much. Light senseless in the blood. Will always wake. But who can wait?

The god can sometimes wait. Hence called "the god."

And that's sleepwalking too. Though not the one sleep paved with that one walking. Not the sleep of wasp and speaking bee. That's sleepwalking: endless time of sun killed in his boat. Time that couldn't end. Yet time that ends. Time whose ends are vinetwined each to each. Between whose grasp of dead wood on the live we may spend every day. If so, then secret stirring in dead wood.

If so, the blood condensed to flower's glazier-flesh bolts gold through death.

And this we know already. We have seen it.

Sleepwalking as when alien sweat encased me. Not the salt of burning sun. The boulder that my furnace still refines, though both are old. Not the sunfat wrapped in rootweave, taken in, crushed down till sun leaks out in spraying rills of fat. That one I know. Tongue turns to lock itself around sweat's signature. Rip out the living lozenge from the hex of salt. Its crystal rank and army of the diamond. Sweat there holds a sentence made of nearly secret words. Like reading picture-alphabet. The toucan has its beak to stretched-out dog. The winnowing fan puts muscled air to river. And the river touches all on top and bottom; and the man with jackal face is at its mouth.

You read the pictures. They're clear. But clear to whom, and when?

Like this the name of sweat. As this, the living eye whose flash is lightning in the salt-sting. But then the sweat was other and I crept in nameless mazes.

Hibou.

Between the beacon's glass and scale of fires that lights it, I saw him dreaming.

We were stripping off the city's thinking-fat. The yellow hardened bulb-out where the city thought about itself. Where it noticed grass come up and had to herd its bladed spray into a tract. Where it burned away the jut of levelled glass with skies rolled out on tracks. We were at those places, all of them. Deposits of the city self-observed. The spring and coral winter of a heat that came in shelves. The terminus, the staves cropped out to fencing. The wire that boils between them and the teeth that they show white to mapping hands.

We were rolling up those fatted mats. Night perched on the huddle of black boxes; night was wetness and the dust could drill a conelight from it. Day bracketed a scum on street pools. We worked at night because the city was forgetting. Not for long, not very much. If we're lucky, long enough to let a knot of day turn brown. To scorch its wheat to palaces where bug horn coughs a clatter rubbed on churning bug horn. In that kind of twisted brown, something could still happen. Pearly wind to roll and roll and roll the day between its weft. Spit to drop a well between the brown day's jamming, and a well that by more nights could crust its sugar shaft. A day like old rope. More like robins' nests, unpicked rope from rope with louse-destroying motion.

Tough black skin cracked around a blackish silver claw.

The claw unfurling consonants from rope's brown meat. Plucking out the letters till they'll lie there flat and smooth. Not quite flat, because all barbed on top with twine's loose music; not quite smooth, because still meshed and woven from a hamstring net. Still ravelled even when the world is most unpicked. Rope is wound upon itself or it is nothing. Between there are degrees. But there's no type and typists' metal grilles don't clamour to a nightly slice between degrees of rope.

The eggs' blue lost to focus. Pile of baby moons.

The bark-carved map caught clean but several layers back. Browner where the rivers start their babble. Or where the babble's washed in muddy cloth. And river-black is cracked across the underground in filigree.

The red quills shocked around dark leather. Sprung against the sky, in first day now, as thinnest bolts. Cherry neon through the lemon gorge that rises on me. Redfruit tart, scratched from its clusters sour as my seeing, and knitted as a windsock. Small tube that catches lemon strafe and, for a moment, drowns it; small thread, and I can write its buzzy sheet across the day. Where acid's young and shallow. Where bruisetoned salve is drying on the night's quick termination.

How couldn't you see day following night –

I don't know how we didn't. Or how I still don't. Even now I hiss in front of buried suns; I break their humming while it's barely built. Even now in night, with day expected, I can clank my backplates. Tense myself into a dog-arch. Guard the morning orange away, back down to where it lay in bitter columns on the dirt. I can do all that now. As long before the morning, and a morning's width and smell before the day.

But still I won't see it coming. I've never really learned to do that. He, the one I dug with, didn't care about the daylight clamping down like furnace thunder. He didn't care if it came soft or vicious to the edge of dark. I mean: it didn't matter to him, as long as he knew how it happened. He just wanted to see. Caring came later, when he had to study all the shapes that rosy air had pressed upon whatever gel remained. Whatever lunar ore. Cooled beyond the cold that any day's aluminium could stand without re-freezing. But night and pasty moons are splayed along a different metal's streaming. You'll know that, I imagine.

I imagine.

And P. who pounds out script. In the furrows of an anthill wreck. Alone inside the green breath of a gabled house. Or never enough alone, with orders in three languages arriving every day on too-clean paper. Never left alone enough by tethers of a many-tethered time and pulled too tight for sounding. E. working with a chisel and hammer on the silver rills that brood around his house.

The truck exhaust in ramparts and the canisters that chatter on their beds.

The vats beneath the street. The inch of rubber skin, licked out to inches' thickness by a mouth that I can't name, hardened with a water that hasn't got much name yet.

And gold enough to engine so-and-so-much abstract thought in gold.

And gold enough to roll away the golden place. To fill its chutes with dirt-creased figures. Sweat become a vein of salt that bristles out of them. No more wetness bred in sweat's clear drip. Only scrimshaw. Writing made of whalebones. Washed dry on every hillock of their faces' shores.

Long cousin to the figure P.'s been beating. Long sister to the steak and flank of drums. Sound punched to its pulp. A sieve that sifts the nodule from the song. Drums flare the fading ghost of polyp-mouths in rows. Pale as things not born to see the sun. Things that, if they live, are always seawaves in the throat. Sitting when a body sits, standing when it stands. When sleeping on your back, the tulips chirrup at the ceiling and the sky if ceiling's torn; when on your front, they scatter through the earth. If on your side, they whistle at each other from a distance. And the tulips pursed on someone else's speech perk up. They've heard this song before.

This is Egypt now. I'm telling you Egyptian. The sinew of it all can slither through your eye-gap if you leave it just the least bit open. And eyes are almost never fully closed.

3rd.

He comes to her arrayed in spires. She's told him: *Come to me the way you come to others. Crack my house and meld it with the god.* His promise is a forked bolt in the squall. Too late to sheathe himself in zinc, too late to wear a lesser vision's armour. Now she waits and counts the star's nap on a grid of outstretched silk. She plots his passage down by Ox and Bear, down by the wheel of ice-locked sparks, the signal tower's pinhole belt.

Too late. Though now she's only seeing thread to thread, now opening the artery of cold to let in arch-built heat. Though now she only rides the room's set course. A pile of altars hiding between her walls. Though now she tracks a shapeless itch. A hand that frets at stale air's weft, held down by gouts of smouldered mint. Of incense and its tattoo in the nostril; of the powder's white-leached rainbow in her mirror.

Already now too late. Too late when rusty crow's cough wrenched her mouth apart and whinged with hollow voice: *You promised that you'd come to me the way you come to sea. You promised that I'd know how zephyr saw, how snorting horses whine to feel your footstroke through the mud.* He heard the living hairs that bent along her voice's cone. And knew that living hairs would soon be dead and locked to final bending. Like the last stem, stiffneck, craned, toward last doomed sun.

The gods don't know the future. And the oracle, who knows, is bound to limp sway by the fret of poison gas. And the sibyl, if she knows, can only gurgle through her flesh-collapse.

But they guess as people guess. So he shines foglight through her dream. On night that laid down billowed sheets. Her eye is black cloth toward the black. Prepared to douse the fiery visit. He promised that he'd come to her like lightning. Like the clang of spindly thrones in thunder's theatre. They've both seen it. Tin-roofed notes of warring bone on bottom reaches of the cloudwarp.

Tin-clad harpies spool their barb beneath his red corona.

Women with tin radiance hold statue-stiff below the clash of thrones.

And the faces in her dream were flat as clay. A dream of Aztecs grooved between the temple steps. Of pyramid that pierces Aztec time. That shoves a windbreak up against the cities' change. The beetles vanish; then they overtake. The beetles swarm along a sea-smeared cliff because they're routed out of beetle groves; then seamilk feeds them hard. A part of them is lined with calcium. A chamber in their black reactors sponges into stone. The one old mouth, the claim of pincer, clicks aside. Now passage leading onto mouth in choirs. The crooked throats left beetle-deep by lava undersea.

Exterminators drive the beetle out and accidentally ensure that Aztec time will end with beetle gods. That future Aztecs know to fear the mouth beneath the mouth. To lay new grain before the pincer and to skitter from the altar. And to kill the beetle's enemy, to drive it through the waves; and then to make it god in turn. Through which new file of coloured bloods the pyramid still sleeps.

Not sleep. The life of rocks. So slow that to a rock's eye there is only brief explosion. And the rock is mad with eyes. New York a fusillade of blinding silver. Cincinnati rustcrop shattering the hills. Kansas City lash of brick and iron, river's dim convulsion. Dallas hell. All California bred from seizure in the coral. Wyoming sudden pits in fitful mud. Wisconsin flood-bit, quick to heal the gash. A squadron under London's horns. A flash of spit through Paris. And some places hardly anything. The killing field that mothered pale Nebraska death to heaps of Juarez murder: flickered brown cones in the stuttered clip of night. A race of scabs come up and shed. The horses halting so alike that rock sees lazy horse-line on the air. A blurry rope of raids that came from nowhere. Came from where the horsemen saw a theatre curve; where the horsemen knew that coral marked its corridor and everyone else went cracked with all the distance.

Arrows bristle out the theatre's neck. Curved wall stitches wall's lip to the sky. And through its streets, seen only by the man who's sewn to horse, moves death that moves like rain. A dome sealed off by thousand drops. Then damp gust. Then the night-grain hollers dry.

The women turn desolate because she tells her dreams. She forces grave-stale breath of dream that rolls in rotting spasm through her skull. She whispers into curtains with a half-smile and the women freeze. Halfway through ripping out their hair, through shattering the jar and vase, through dragging sharpened fingernail down chest. She has the big cat's onyx underneath her sight. Her sockets bloom with touch of puma. And the women know how women go to fire. Know how the lightning's screw will tear new threads inside her. How the screw's old path will strip. Leave twists of silver on the floor. How floorboards plan with household wind to leave the shearing thread in board-slat; and how city's blood congests with ruined parings.

She leans over the curved arm of the couch.

She leans against the inside of the doorway with one arm extended and her planed face turned away.

She crouches by the window and makes gesture of the loom. Turns window's thread of glass-struck light between her little fingers. Jerks her head around to see if someone's watching; when they are, stares at their staring, but not at their eyes.

Pretends to read. Pretends to eat. Pretends to number goldflakes in the portrait.

Then the brightness of him comes to kill.

¶

Lantern. Where the sackcloth wants to glow. A prism. A blank of spotted planes, clear but spotted and with rippled light, where cloth can refine its fire. A cloth's edge hums with birdfire, nightfire, fire of blackened forest. Black fire amulets that sleep inside a shank of savaged wood. Cloth climbs into lanterns when it wants to draw these things. Trace its inner tracings on the world; char night along the spires of its vocabulary; perform surgery on itself. Sackcloth dreams all darkly, with a terror smile for worlds passing overhead. The worlds' thin bottom layer dapples cloth with water ingots where it's dreaming.

In the dream a man made out of cloth is performing a medical operation. He's the surgeon and the patient. He sticks needles in himself and leaves them there. They bristle in the operating wind. Air minted grey with medicine sweeps over his new mane of reeds. They clatter out bright words. But now is not their time and the cloth man can't record them. When he's anaesthetized, and skinned with grey hard veins to ease the cutting, he dips into his gut. His hand unravels on the burlap weft of stomach walls. On the other side it snaps again to shape. To prod and crawl and flicker. There is an inch of loose thread for his wrist. If it were pulled tight, his hand would be abandoned to his stomach. He'd have to walk inside the scream. Ripping out a melon from his seeding grounds. That other dream. Always second dreaming. Some dreams, called *lanterns*, never make themselves appear; they hijack first dreaming and burst up through its skin. Parasites exploding from a blister.

But the tunnelled screaming passes over cloth man. And with his hand unravelled, he pulls up shapes of writing from his belly. Runes of scorch. They have brittle skins that pigeon off into the breeze. But underneath that coating, they're wrought-iron. And cloth can lay them over peopled cities. Make people seize around them in the daytime. See the people's hands rake through their hair. Where new black letters block the path. See the people fold their glasses and unfold their papers. See their backpacks dotted on an empty square. They've abandoned it to writing not their own. They sometimes hide in vacant storefronts on the square. To watch it. To study its movements.

Butterflies and sooty doves land on the twisted wrack of lantern-writing. The letters are still and soundless while the bugs pick over them. While the birds arrange themselves to birdlumps.

Then there's an iron whining in the sky. Like last tails of an air raid siren. And then a heaving metal crunch; and then the bird or butterfly is gone, and the letter is new grey with stolen feathers. New orange and blue and pink with butterfly fans.

Lantern fish. A fish that's learned to write like lanterns write. Suppositious. None have been seen. Or at least no one has survived the seeing. They are conjured up by hidden hurricanes. Spoken softly underneath the roar that tends our darkest water. Time is a waiting for them. Among the things that time is waiting for, lantern fish are right there, snapping. The *city* is a hedge against them. It collects a grain of writing and distributes it between the furrows. Furrows pre-exist the city and are wounded by it sometimes. Lantern fish aren't the only objects of the city's safety, but they're definitely one object. Definitely a rider on the margin. Where stencilled bears are barking clumsy letters like Cyrillic. Where paper dogs cry Asian characters that look like ornate golden houses. And where the lantern fish is waiting for the lashing of its speech. The grove of poison whips that, if they come, will come to tear apart a city. And form another in its wreck. This is characteristic of the city: that in falling off the world, it breeds ten thousand future cities in its fossil. It must also, then, be a quality of the lantern fish. As one of the quick dreams that cities bank against.

We can see the fishes' silhouette turn courses by an undersea volcano. We can wait for the eruption. But we can also look around the slag that's piled up from the last volcano's spit. And find in it an augury of lantern fish. Their writing. Find it curled into the tendrils of a dead old god. Who dreams there with a statue cased around him; who may be himself the statue. Sometimes this god will be a *lantern*. Worlds slide over his sleeping in the same way. His little murder-smile turns up the same small corners of his mouth. His grey teeth are pounded ash in capsules. Just like the rest of him. And when they show in dreamy smiling, then the world that's sliding over feels him. He comes up through its wells. He makes a floor for all that world's new song, and singers tumble down it. He puts a noisy mould along the corners of its bread. He knocks over plastic castles in its fishtanks.

When the dead god smirks up through your world, through the grating on your sewers, it may be the time of the lantern fish. Run.

To another world if one is near. If not, there's nowhere to run. You'll have to crouch and babble till the city falls, then fit yourself into a city grown up from it.

Lanyard. Thin. Danger's clanging at the end of one. The lanyard turns destruction into poses. The breaking act is held in whatever way your body learns to freeze. There's a standard for these freezes. No one can meet it. And people know that, so they tolerate all failing; but they put bad seeds into your guilty chamber. Into their own. The seed becomes a hanging dial of flesh that flutters in our throats' rear hollows. This is all the lanyard's fault. Not really. This is all a fault held on the lanyard. That's more accurate. You see how lanyards, even just as things to talk about, make fault a new red question. At the lanyard's end is danger, hanging like a cowbell. When we stand close together, danger clangs together and we moo. Make a baying toward the muffled sundown.

Lap. Smallest form of ocean. A cave that sprouts a tongue to lick itself. The motion of this tongue when someone's listening. Paddle sounds, sounds of waterbugs that skate along the pool's most solid glass. The different panes of glass that stack up in the water; the moment they bend up toward a marriage. Water with a glassy skin in layers, and a shapeless hulk asleep for all of time beneath it. Calm now. Lap is also in the man who crouches where this water's seam is slipping from the land. Where this water's finger tweaks the seashell rows.

Lap is this man's activity. His attempt to catch the water sound and stitch it in a word. His watching of the skater bugs, his winnowing of limbs until they're thin enough that he can skate, too. The blue and greyish China that rolls through this man's evening. The yellow Italy, with abalone muscled white, that chatters wiry music when he looks at it. The casement of an unglassed window. The clap of gallops that remains behind a horse. When day starts draining out and night prepares its microscope, hooves will jangle far away. The man will look into their prints. He'll see the crest of dirt that hooves have banked to shape; he'll see the dirt's rubbled margin when it threatens to fill in the hoofprint. There will be a wind tuned to his branches and his hair. Cameras move out wide; sound recorded live on site. When we watch the man, we're lapping. And lap is in his face. When he can stand with no expression, walk away. Look back with no expression. And with no expression run into the hills that evening etches on the skyline.

Also, lap: a kind of vehicle that brings the world to you. When riding in a lap, the world brings out its pipes and nozzles. They stand before you in a copse, like choirs of copper fruit. You can do anything with them. The lap, as vehicle, doesn't tell you how to act. Every nozzle, every pipe is workable; it can produce a precious breed of water, or suture through the wind inside a house. But you can also bang on them, ride them like seesaws, carve a language from their shapes and learn to speak it. You can know that they are cities; you can follow them to cities that they touch. You can graph the pipes' whole network. In this form, the predator of lap is a mirror. When laps carry you by mirrors, you'd better close your eyes. Or the pipes will look too flat, and you'll wonder what you're doing. If it's right. If anyone who saw you would understand; if the people seeing you now are on your side. You'll wonder if there are sides at all.

In the mirror, another lap and rider catch the angle of your wondering. They do it wrong. But words like "wrong" undo the lap. Its transportation vanishes. And you're small and softskinned in a house that creaks to strangers' steps. In a house whose walls have curved and puffed around the clouds of strangers' breathing. Watch out.

Hibou.
Wherever the drawings are –
At least, wherever we find drawings –
There we also find the water.

Water's prong, its lash and trail of fingers, gathered by the drawing claw. A mass of pigment. Dusted hard like felt. The pointing man who rises from the amber's clouded glass; the buffalo whose speed is streaked along a crystal batch of liquor; the instrument, sound-mixing bowl held distant by a neck spined out with pegs. All of them draw water. We could hear the skritch and smoothing sound of chalk that cleaves to chalk. And in its grainy drift, there was a numbering of rivers. Pebble-freeze and hiccup on the broadplaned wall: a way to count the sea.

The glide of chalking hand selects. It carves one sea stone from another, makes them show a splitting rind. Where turquoise water melted once with gold; where water's toothy sapphire found a mesh of teeth with silver. The raised face of the drawing is volcano talk. Volcano coming forward from that land its rain set down. The god-deep song that makes a city's edge: taken all at once, it seems too much for music. Seems too much built out, too lined with foreign reeds and wickered steel. And this is true. There is a breath inside that seeming, loaded with an atlas of new heats. The girder in the sun is not the sun on lipped aluminium. The sun that mats the dogfur is a different one from suns who strip the dead grasshopper cask.

And their rhythm, when the sunswath folds and focuses, is all a different rhythm. Spot bright-filtered by horizon. The train of spots that wheels around an eyeglass. When sun bears down around a beam of stones, it's dangerous to beat the broad-sun rhythm. You'll find yourself a hollow zone where sun-rock springs wild shoots. You'll want to lay and spread but find that spreading locked in columns' hex, become a hissing magnet where the capitals cut time. Scroll-rolled column tops let down a blinding net. And only with the glinting lava song, the song whose scope of aeon will be taken for a pause, can you learn to swim that net.

The rattle-chute stays pregnant in your chest. The scuttered rocks sit perfect in the notches of your spine. Each bonestar gnarled up yellow-white to give the sunstone's throne. You –
and I and we –

recline upon a chain of thrones. We bend along the tangent of a throneworks. And when we crack, the nape-nerve's knot uncoiling from the neck, our cracking is an interrupted throne. A change of gold, like sea change in our frames.

And just as serious. The bone of sleeping coral: no less serious than sunstone shuddered from its throne, called vertebra. The Greek-dreamt wall of gold and mottled white is register of bone that found its metals; the fretwork monster gold, the golden furnace, is a melting-ground of spines come bent and loose. We've learned this now. We know where gold will go when it has shivered through our flesh. And with its edges square, with string-hole punched out of its centre, know you hold a chain of sea-bone where the focused light once played. To give some shape to time; to bury shapes, seed burrowed in the brain, that later look like codes because we can't look at them dead on. Too bright. The crust of black-fried iris, crumbled eye-scale falling toward the wind like ashy petals.

From the molten fix beneath the sea, volcano water muscled into shape, a ridge of thrones crops Earth from end to end. Beneath the continent, the ship and ship-scared dragon. Beneath the whale and cloud of plankton buzzed in whalesight. A ridge of thrones as knots of black gold spine.

From there to cities' highest peak: a shaft of heavy water. Called in one place *light warm rain*. In another place, *abyssal plain*. The seabed rolls with glowing eggs that sign a phosphor music to the stars.

A hundred years ago, they wrote that someone said: *We are the plant.*

And half as many gone, that someone else: *Whenever we find these drawings, we find water at not more than 6 feet.*

The sea cat cocks his horns at me. Air ripped out into a portal and the sea cat pads on tide-wet sand. His steps pronounce a tongue-flick and a hiss: *lynx. Lynx.* He cocks his horns to etch a cursive on the salt of tideborne air. And then he nods, retraces, nods again. The wave is full of grapemeat and the rocks adhere behind him. All focus of the day's last dimness drawn around the cat who carries night. Who shines a disc of moon between his horns and spends the day in feeding on gold discs. Planted footswidth underneath the brass-veined dirt. At height of big cat's head around the bursting stalks of field edged out with copper. The field holds in a copper basin and the sea cat shifts his supple engine through it. Swats away the beetle. Lets the dragonflies be wreath of arrows on his head.

And now the sea cat nods and pulls a focus to his shape. The day shaved into night-drink on his black fur where it's marbled through with orange. And where he nods, a rivulet of flashing water nods back from the rocks. Then a stream. Then a brook. And then a river, sea's claw pushing seawall up between them. River bearing quick blood on its surface and a dust of bronze tornados on the bottom. Behind a wall of shells and frozen seafans, so the river will be fresh and ocean salt.

Sea cat nods at me and I lie face-up on the river. Sky now bronzed and woven with a moss of browning rushes. The river's metal hardens into thin platform beneath me, plate of gold-blotched blood atop its quicker cousins. Blood that holds in vine-weave while the river's blood still tumbles.

Sea cat nods and I begin to take the river's course.

I don't close my eyes. I keep them open. Watch the river's edge in blurring with the edge of soft-domed sky.

still Hibou.
Larktree
  grackle lamp
    broken mirror
      strings in shoulder-hinge
        music of Ecbatan.

Screech falls like a bandage from the lark tree. White-grained strip of unoiled bird. And hard glint, rub of birds' machinery. The spokes that undergird a lark's brief chute of throat are dry within a cutting wind. Moved air turns to sandcrust on their turn of mottled steel. Air-fleck caught between the patches in the finish; grey on colder grey, metal grass that fingers through a different metal's field. The outer edge is lead. The horizon is a curving slash of lead. Half-circled where the Earth burns through a rank of sunspot ghosts. Where the outer world's edge makes white fire against its blurring. Grinds its marble roof against the feather-flame to keep itself a circle. And as the flint that scrapes quick on the marble: screeching spokes arrayed within the lark.

When the lark is dead, a separate air will wave its spokes. Zephyr's size and hugging push toned down. Zephyr's mist, the wet that boils like static in its walls, now wrenched out of the bead. No more maze of water drops. Now a water turned to wind. No oil-sheen and no fogblot on the skin. But hollow drink inside a hollowness. Wind that wets a throat you carry somewhere hidden, fills a pouch reserved for secret food. Cold rips down the paper flowers in bud – but in the spidermap of river-blood that puts touch into your fingers, taste between your teeth, the cold wind's dryness lies down for your feeding.

I have not watched myself drink it. But I know that when I do, I arch my spine, and spine-strung ribs hang jackalwise above. The narrow dog drills through my face's soil. The narrow wolf-dog mange sprouts ear behind my ear. Tongue beneath my tongue for different lapping. Teeth gone nipping-short and teeth stretched out to curve around a neck.

My eyes are thinner and see less. But what they see, they see faster than before. World snapped into crescents made of speed. All move like I've been dreaming. Move in a direction that I know they will, that couldn't have been any other way – but if I try to know why I know, the speed-sight shatters. Then a mobile of blank arcs. Arrows bent and scorched and hanging from the wire that brings the rain. And I'm alone. And I howl.

Alone among the rabbits and the tree-speed tattooed on their roots.

All in this other wind. Mate of Zephyr, called Apeliota.

Her sickle taps for dull spots on my shell. Click and click. Until the bark-held thud sounds back, and Zephyr's mate has found a cave to coil in.

Apeliota, Zephyr latch the larksquawk to its season. One to puff their growling sacs. The other then to clang what brittle reeds they leave when season's out. When they've dipped and blinked in flying to the same tree, half an earth away. Lark eyes dart a scalpel through the thinnest well of time, down to where the world is black-scoped crawl of vegetables and gods, then out the other side. Back up through the iron, silver, bronze. The dirt made rich with untapped liquor and the dirt made rich with dying. Past a backbone curved and fluted big enough to bear the city's roof; past a hundred million backbones small enough to mount a human skull. All lark to the season. And their dry stalks are for Apeliota's hand. Only finger long enough to winnow out the delicate clash. Slip between the fibre of a lark's stone throat and pluck the echo-thread. Dead lark cage become a harp beneath her nails.

Lark tree sways with a glissando, notes that hang to melt so metal can build up inside the cloud, when she runs her wristbones down its length.

As when another tree hives out in grackled bud. And grackle mouths have to carry the whole animal they eat for. Bird wet down until it's only wisps of meat. A quiver-pile of tendons to provide the mouth with turret. Openwork shaft like an oil derrick. Like a TV signal tower. Strung complete with ligaments that prop the mouth to let it be a satellite. Support too frail for seeing. But strong enough to keep the evening grackle-hoarse.

Strong and strange enough to shake the power from a streetlight when they cawed right at its base. I've seen that.

I have seen the oilwrapped root go sponged and twitchy in the dirt. I have seen the light's white nerves just before they disappear. Light-root lost to firmness. So the nodes fall from each other, break the circuit, break the circle of their music. And the light that is a brain –

And the brain that's made of rivers –

And the rivers that will flood you as a light –

Snap off. There is a clap of locust cough. Shelled flesh when dust has caught along its mouth. Sound of interrupted snore, snailcurve of the nose that pulled too hard against itself. Something pink flaps shut. Something quiet rises from the night where streetlamp's riverlight had kept it silent in the evening. I hear a mass of dry wings marching and I see the gold and bronze that filigree the wings' now-empty husk.

So there is another depth of night because the grackles shrieked and bubbled. I have seen this. I have seen it more than once.

Tonight I shuffle on their city's edge; expect that I should see it once again.

Now the season of the larks has weathered last degree of sunbake. And the sun in tree-set arbours turns to iron. Day is browned enamel baked to gold on risen banks of the city's leaves; and lark-screech rolls back up for coming freeze. Soon the grackles mount that bank. Soon the wire hisses with its moorings in a ruin. And soon the wire-whipped spark will drive its shockwhite planes into a breeze that cupped a stillness.

From the pits, percussion rises. Blasting cap inwoven with the gust. Tonight again is called tonight. I strafe my face along the building-pits. The earthworks where they raise a coral rose. Oyster moon rolls on its petal. Scaffold-rose, stem barbed with wooden slats, dark feet between the rungs to scurry toward their flower. Where now, in Egypt, comes the desert cold. The water blades uprooted from the sand; the air like panes of glass across long wastepile. The air like panes of glass between a desert and its water, where the water pools when day has drawn it out. Look up. See water's turn along the face you cannot see. See water bodies formed and broken on the sheet.

And hear the sand-fed root, the root that gains no grasp, talk sand-rasp with the water's empty whistle. Hear the slipping root slip off its rock. The rock that hoards its seam beneath the sand, the sand that gives no green meat to the root. Hear the tendril hand uncurl. A husking sound. A sound of corn torn from the silk. Of leaves that Zephyr's ravish tears from tree.

A sound of locust from the shell, cicada from the shell. Dead skin sliding over living. Dead skin hardened to the envelope of time that birthed this moving lump of horns. Live wing's veining slipping under dead. Empty veins cough out the full ones' future. Vessel drained to mark the season's suck. All dry in turn, till finally the last wet flies the vein-wall and the locust drowns in sand. The cicada's poison shriek is hammered loose. Cicada venom rolling in the sandstorm.

Cicada drink undrinkable and still no other water. But the water on the desert roof receiving broken stars. Cracked transmission, absent letter, wire of quick thin heat that won't give up the word within. Heated in the coil and tube of star-set. Warp of radiations in the high unfalling water. Disease of drinking off the desert roof. There are stories and we've heard a few of them. Someone had to tell us why we shouldn't drink that water. Otherwise we'd roll up desert steps, our weak backs to the blow, and drain all star-wrong water from the glass. Feel it plump the vein with buzzing worms; feel the wasp stamp wasp-house from our stomachs.

Water is the tread where one sun sinks its shattered radio.

The other water, fountain from the ground, is full of ground-sun's growl and grind and bellow. When we drink it we can hear the iron tube. We can hear the mole-wrack left in hollow land. The falling slates of water's roof that clang around our feet. And say: tonight there's too much coming from the star.

Tonight the star is hot with evil speech.

Tonight the star wants enemy to drink.

Tonight the star's in coils that shock us when they're wet.

Tonight the star's back panel snaps and furnace cracks its wall.

Tomorrow night, we'll say: There used to be a star.

That's the way of building Egypt. I want water. But the water is the final zone of rest. For everything, for spider-drape, for hornet armour, fur within the sand. For poison rock and rock still rich with milk. For cream of death, for cream of flesh, for cream that lights the rose with petal pearl. Build a spiral out of bronze-shot bricks and study where the stagnant pool is breeding. Do it first. Or else the stagnant flood will be mosquito eggs strung through your brickwork clay. Mosquito egg in planting sod and rat tooth through the delicate foundation.

Percussion comes up from the pits; which means tonight could be a women's night. It is. Tonight they won't be cats or crop of birds. They'll retract and peck the grass with seeing feet. They'll rip the lid from sole-eyes and walk down through fathom's mud. To see the gasping fish, the metal bugs, the shards of pottery that missing Egypt cured until they balled up into music.

Tonight the women make a pillar walk. The women are a column bristled out with night-close eyes. As close to me as night's blue fibre. Banded where the night will snap it tense.

Tonight the women wander at the edge.

Where column is a magnet of dead gods while living ones still grow up from the pit. Still gain their girders' shape, their skins of lead, their eyes between the frost on glass. The women can ignore them for tonight. They can walk in circles toward the column-place, the circle marked with bright black rock where women's circles tend. And see small life in black rock's oil reflection. See the shrimp egg, louse egg, flickered fish. Old gods stay inside the column; they won't wreck the work of Egypt. But tonight the women walk insensible to Egypt. In the daze of old construction.

I can see them turn to white stone on the lawn.

I can see the sand-choked root crawl up their stone to vein it red.

Away from this. Now closer to the ocean.

The place where old man's iron gets the voices. Voice would spoil in desert water. Too much star condensed in pigment pricks. Too much Saturn grin and too much Neptune chrome. Too-hard peaks of Neptune's metal wave, where metal ocean answers to this ocean made of everything. Neptune crest where voice will break. Reflect away, to rumble in red dust. To meet the ore of old stone gods in sunbelt. Shaken down to molten stuff with old gods' heads beside it. Voice has not survived in other places. Voice can maybe not survive anywhere but here. And the old man's iron is pressing-plate for voices. They arrive on him and leave their pattern etched. They draw a spark of carvings from inside the iron hulk and old man speaks them. Says sometimes:

"Return through spiteful Neptune, lose all companions."

Which is how I know about the ocean's plates. The plates that here are engines under time; that there are thrash and ruin, hard to penetrate. Too dense for moving voice. The ocean's smallest water still is overthick for voices.

I found a broken mirror and I hung up shards of it where old man stands. To let him catch the light-gasp and the secret sea of light. The moment's flood. To give him small bright music in the wind, when mirror talks. To give him total music in the shape. To let the constellation breathe, so no one voice can craze his metal down.

Klang.

In Ionia was strong singing. Full chest holler of the walls cropped white and gold. Ionia in uprights, stilted struts. In cars' back faces gone white with the night. Ionia was blast of marbled bleach and gold that fingered through it. Gold was the vine. White was the plate, the armour, the enamel. People like shaved rocks. People planted at the seacoast and the sea a foam-veined roof beneath their staring. Squarish legs drawn from the people's stone: not separate from its backing, but two thigh-turns blossoming from salt with salt-slab still between them. Insistent harmony. Always pulling up the rose to gleam above their choirs. Always the rose became colossus, petal-light in tower of blooming. Night an empty velvet by the rose's song-nicked walls. They aimed their singing at the blemishes to heal them; but the song would waver, note that followed its own sharpness or that bent to touch the flat, and another dented scratch would cut the rose.

In Ionia is rose's constant maintenance. The people all half-hewn out of their rock and the sea half-still to face them. Foam tendril on the searoof like a dust of blizzard snow. But cliffs of water still beneath the snow-whip. Crusts and peaks of ocean held in place. Wobbled with the people's wobbled song. Not meant to tremble, never, but of course still touched with trembling. The triad banked, the empty octave, sentry notes to make the tower. Open shaft of sentinels, of steel's rung clapped to steel, and the grills more delicate above them.

Under roofs of ocean's frozen knot, the water furrowed faster to make up for its still surface. Water's massive turbine. Fish embalmed in hurricanes with fish-eye rolling silver blink at shoreline. Whales immobile in the drift. Dead octopus on shoreline's dropping slope; its trunk stayed put, but tentacles were wheeling in the water's heavy chop. A spotted cask that had been octopus. Seaflower tangle jabbering above it like a drowned girl's hair in stormdrain.

As the lilies on Ionia's unmoving ocean top. Frozen in the sculpted wave. Melted to its vein and choppy segment. Waves like lead and leaden lilies stuck upon them. But inside the iron barrel of the sea, lily arm dragged screech across the shallows.

The Ionians still tended to their rose.

Didn't see the ocean's bottled thrash.

Soap and bones
Soap and bones
Sing me now what I heard then. Reach down the tunnel's reedprint wall. Sing me now what's tossing in the hollow stone. Cobble in my skull worn smooth by sugared thought that laps against it. Grey rock mouths that close by decade. Lipped and webbed when sugar finds its weave. Sing me. Finally a membrane: skin of smaller mouths to stop up stonehole. Not lightfast.

Not lightfast; so behind it break the shadow waves in miniature, quick clay models of the shadow waves that break above it in my skull's blue canopy. Models of the wave that licks and shudders down the length of time when I reach back to hear the song: soap and bones.

I lie here and I drill through fifty miles of softpacked earth. Pull the skins and fragments from my sieve; pull the backbones and the amethysts that clatter in the cone of my remover. I sort them sometimes. Sometimes by name, so that Sapphire runs beneath the wooden arc of Ship. Horizon ribbed with bronze-worn staves, and sapphire sun above it, mounting day with frozen purple lightning. Sometimes I sort them by the order of my digging. They become new animals. Boned in a line, laid out corpse-flat. Each item is a organ where their bodies' shake is hardened into music. A chunk of flint, two cattails downed with patchy fur, a coin with a hole punched through its centre. I find the parts that time embalmed and dig them up a new assembly.

The dirt, cut into ribbons now, will brook a string beneath them. It will know to have a seizure when someone strums the animal I've made. And it will know that each new object is a node, the gold divisions on a string, where seizure climbs into a chisel-note of bronzed ice.

Where the chisel snaps through facial bone. And its breaking-note pronounces: *king*. And for a moment, middle air is still behind one long white note. One spike of killing music. Or the spike that cracks a sinus so we'll know what killed it first.

The Heaven is unchanged; the dirt-low air still heaves by century; the airless knot of hidden suns won't breathe a different wind. Still solar wind, the ripple only of heat. And still no gust to plump a lung around. But the middle air is ivory around that chisel-note. Its rough parts show their ruffles in a patch of white crests. Its smoothness holds the room in long pearl arcs, in rib-vaults that can lock you in a corner. If there were time, you'd palm the whole new cave and leave your skin-oil where the ivory would take it. You'd sound the world for depths of blue that show up faint on surface-white. A magnet blotted red would pull from abalone curves, and though you couldn't really see it, you would light a row of fires and sleep beneath them.

Spear-sharp trees grow black against the fire's grown blackness. A row of thin forked branches set around the fire-kept circle.

Your letters may break with the telling. You may have to carve out new ones where the bone tells you: I'm soft. Or dowse for soft banks set on hardness. Piles of damp balled dust that barely coat the secret of a horn. Your work may be to find where horns are sleeping. If the horn can ever sleep. Your work may be to find where horns have always crouched awake and help them split the bone-roof. Help horns beneath tense temple grind against the skin.

The horn's a waiting eye. And eye-worlds wait to wrap around horned letter.

Chisel-work pronouncing *king – king – king*. And night a web of red-walled dark where scraps of alphabet still quiver in the horns you haven't found.

Like but different from the dark I rifle through. The dark condensed in wet black earth. I tunnel it to find the song that used to sing me *soap and bones. Soap and bones.* And where the tunnel's wall is thin as one-grained sheets of dirt, I see the god-shaped animals in hunting. They almost never seem to sleep. This far down, they may have ripped the sleeproot out and licked its sap into their hunt. Found the knot of tired fibres; pressed its amber on their skin and known where dream is quiet in the daytime. This far down, there isn't night or day.

I see them tall as awe; I huddle, bound with limbs, when they've brought down a crashing prey.

When the crash is hard enough, it throws my chipping-hand against the whorls of bone. I sit; I try to stand; I see a letter growing where my chisel tapped the wall. Thrown weight of one dead god is like a compass for my letters. If we waited long enough, we'd be tossed around enough to hollow out an alphabet. Thirty letters in a hundred years. A hundred hundred more to see where they had pads and breeding-skin. To know which ones would stick to others' juice, which ones would knit or slip or chatter.

That could be a method.

But the day or night is long. I've got to work.

And there are letters I could never find that way.

There are letters shaped like nothing that I toss away with bone-scurf. Only later notice them: a galaxy of crab and coral poking through the dust.

The song called "soap and bones" was not a letter song. I have to find it all at once or let it die.

Came husking over cobbles, singing soap and bones. Leather shift on rock-knobs where the pigeon seed was lost. Sole's low cough between the mortared pebble. Smooth worn smoother with the shuffling songs like "soap and bones." Rock-soft birds that clotted in the rocks' grey sea and didn't move when Soap-and-Bones came singing. They pecked and stepped between his legs. They glossed themselves with feather-butter. Oil encased with yellowed brown and safe against all feet.

Look up. Pigeons fly to bend the pigeon wave. Pigeons sit and waddle when the song puts streamcreep low between the cobbles. Iron cones put steam into the day, to ease its dying, and the pigeon weather pumps a new fat shape to dodge the steam. Pigeon cloud trails streamcloud. At their border, mane of stars. A strip of friction's tinsel cutting goldfleck from the fallen afternoon. Soap-and-Bones sat under all of this. The crust and wet-web of his leather made their crinkled jump to catch the pigeon breeze. The breeze of steam.

Day above them all a fatty tissue. Worked under by chalk fingers. Fingers flaked and pruned with soap. Morning's ghost returned to pulp and sound the evening clot. Stretched white hands like candlewax that push the pigeon tumour toward its mouth of exit-skin; that press the tumour balled from steam until it shatters into salt beneath the flesh. Work the shrug of milk, the blood-pearled knot. Prepare the work of night's blue teeth, so day will lie around the city in a drifting set of ribbons. Then the night can tooth them down, run bared jaw over evening's granite wall.

And when I step into the night, I'll be shocked against its shoreline. Feel the water-day recede, its cold flit down my middle, feel it seek the new ravines. New space that night will come eroding from the hollow shells that wait for it. The place where skin like bugsheath made hard domes to block a sinkhole: night burns scalpel through their paper plies. Nightbeast has to have a well. For lying flat inside. For cleaving to the dirt and patting bouldered dust to level. For listening to thunder roll inside the world; for having rabbit fur prick up when hanging lightning strikes the underground.

Rabbit feels when lightning's fork is rifling through the roots. Rabbit feels when lightning's sheet moves white above the blue-blanched grass that hangs down from the underside of Earth. And knows the inner sun has met a turning; knows the inner moons are drawing down, finding lightning-shaft to bring them to the seas. Down in secret earths where down is up. Toward the ground that secret-faces ours.

And where the secret water gathers, rootdrink pulps it for its seeds of carried moon. Our ocean's jet turns bright and thin with moonseed.

Feel the root-talk buzzing in the bare skin of my feet.

So Soap-and-Bones came riding down the pavement.

And the cornice-flies were quiet in their walk; and the cornice-rats stopped scratching through the bark. No more inner house today to gnaw free of this house. No more blonde-striped building wood beneath an inch of whitewash. Rats were quiet for the singing man, their tails tense as fine instruments. Needles turned to scritching out another kind of earthquake.

Rattails sweep the grains of bottle glass.

Whisht, whisht. Live birth of a constellation:

Do not farm under this sign. Do not set your lands in order. The ox is taken by strange pains. The heron claws a water-bulge and finds it unbroken. When the building burns, do not put out the fire; when the burning wagon passes, let it pass. It goes into a hall of night that you cannot prevent.

The seed of this season is tinted glass. The fruit of this season is glass ornaments like ovaries and tubes. The meat of this season is a slice of flesh that lies rusty by the rusted pot.

Expect a drought. Expect a lash of murdered hair to bring the rains. Expect the victim to be young and sideways, hair's black curtain red-streaked in the roof's front gutter.

Don't let the cow calf. You haven't got the tool that can quiet its bent offspring. The dog will sniff and growl when cows are near, because the dog will see a bloodvine hanged from canopy of cows when night is empty. Trust the dog. If the cow gives birth, the calf's cord will have pustules, each one grown around a too-big tooth. Scoop out the teeth and plant them in a ruined place. Don't go back after the planting. Direct your enemies to sleep there. They won't die, but they will forget whatever they'd wanted from you.

The Heaven looses eight new folds of darkness.

The Hell is hot in groundwater.

The Middle Air is tough and damp.

Pray to half-seen men and animals that aren't acting like they should. Pray to trees that vanish. Pray to horse-eyes' black that glitters and goes dull. Pray where rabbits are a silver meat and comb through sheaves of moonglow.

When the child stares from the field's edge, don't stop him. But tell him later: There was danger. Ask the child: Did you feel it? He may lie. He felt it.

Dome-light hatched behind the membrane cloud. Veins as a newborn bird. The spread of light is pulsing there, where cloudvein blocks its entry. We look up into light's egg and we notice where its fluid turns to flesh. Where delicate white water wraps a muscle form, where yolk has grown an eye that sprouts deep root inside the sunswath. We know it with a knowing made of music. That nerve-twist, cage gone down to twine around a cage, is feeling through a peopled underbrush. That canebrake opens, one side swayed to strophe of the other side in swaying. So the nervetree wrought from everything can plant. So light can swim into the eye as well as swimming from it: a bulb that holds an ocean shape, that keeps a line but sets the line to currents. What pricks the line to gaps: we call it "bird." What wrecks the line and forces it through soil, to kiss the metals, tongue the brace of seeds: we call it "storm." You can hear the copper kiss where S and T slip sparks.

You can see a cavern of the world lit up with copper streaks and know that storm has come, to drive the light into a pouch where light can breed.

The same way you can see a song called "soap-and-bones." Hear "soap" begin – and boneflakes drift down eddied air to graze the wooden floor. Hear "soap" in ending – cleanest river-milk has clipped medallions from the stream. They were sleeping in the river. Slept until a word dove down to fathom out their shape.

71

3ʳᵈ.

No sound but that it stalks with mystery. The big-cat walk leans padfoot over matted tines of grass. Picks bowl-note, bell-note, amber chime from where the herb is bristled. No mystery but that it trails black air behind the sound. And sound's long body pocked with sucker-marks where toothless mouth of ghost has siphoned blood. Long body trailing long limp ghost through fadeout.

The breathing cloud composed of golden flies. All breath clipped short but luminous. A beaded light. Distributed among the quick-winged nodes. Each organ of its shining veiled with wingbeat; knot of muscled shield between the haze that hovers. Write erratic movement on the breath. Comes out in arctic knives, pure falling arch across the room that sound has shaped beneath its hint. Live breath drains over currents of the air gone floodplain-dull. Live breath incised the ridge from stonepacked mud, cut through the stonecrop's softened block and left a group of stags erect and shaking. Deer drain off the needle in the rock. Drink quiver of the flood's recall through eyeless hoof and balljoint. Bone through wire through flesh veneer through rose-scarred nap of fur. Stretch out the bonemouth to a shake that left its floodprint on the granite.

Beginning of an alphabet. The night when pictured man shakes off his head and walks. When pictured man turns loose beneath the heat of all the men he's meant to be. Turns heart and sinew to an oil of tinctured man. And follows print that river's chopped through limestone. Through the hills it also carved, through the etch of snake-spine rubble that it laid between the mountains.

Writing seeps out of the river.

Writing coils within the clang of water's fold. Each ply of river furls the peopled scratch into a world of writing-sites. A world that river turns at will to pale young dough.

Earth and faster gods still ask permission of the water.

Then sound on tape. A sound condensed to shapeless script. The congeries of bats are sliced away. At first. The hieroglyph on iron's shiny face. The whine of needles curling through their winding paths: a tape like river-system, tape's eye downed with spider tributaries. Needle has to plumb them for its song. To dowse the dustwreck for a hint of nightmare water. Where the river's claw injected flood to crawl through bad dust dreams. Has to sound for spider's spike-foot through the dirt that lies on dirt. Five kingdoms down through dirt's repose. The mime of missing river; keepsake mannequin of streams.

In that place, buried bone gets no clear rest.

Black crow-rot never turns to ivy's pulp. Black tide of sores along the antler's crook cannot take antler down to hang above the dead house. Man collapsed will never feed the brass lianas. Man upright will be no safety for a food that death releases. In that place, there is no field of mouths to send the crushed dog's fruit into the city not yet risen. City's root can get no dogjuice in its marble. Put no swath of blood-wild fur across the eye of ivory. Its teeth stay unborn yellow gum. Its arms stay starfish limp, still only dream of arms before the armed beast rises.

The root won't fold on root to make a brain. The city is a heap of polished stones without the written slash that makes them magnetize.

It would appear. To look at tape, it might appear. But it isn't.

Because the tape is bred for tape-head. In its iron lives a cataract of bats. Unkillable unlike the bats before. Can stay alive like virus. All life held in every cell. So rip the batwing, put a puncture through bats' leather: nothing dies. The sound will crumble. Trumpet's metal curl away from columned breath as once it curled around the breathing. Cymbal's seizure turns to hum. The drum coughs speechless, the string stays pegged between the knee and leg of thirst-dead cricket. And they live. The tape has made them live in all their parts. In parts at all; in parts not theirs. When they've gone under red corrosion, then the rusted patch of tape where they once sounded is their life. The silence of a nothing captured sounds much different than the silence of a something lost. You'll know it. Both your temples start to lunge with buzzing. Start to feint at meat's escape. And then you say: *A cymbal lived here. And still lives.*

Be gentle with the cymbal-meat. It hardly holds to bone with all that hum.

The city's cluster, colony of glass-sac lungs, learns space from replayed tape. Learns how to be a city, not just pebbles in a line. Learns that planting pebble seeds the dirt with pebble's rock-shaped dreams; and that the city rises far above its rooftop. That the dream is hidden fruit within the building. That the building's skeleton is charged with nectar and all cities build their upper vault from nectar's sculpted sugar.

Above the city hangs the city. Just as city hangs below itself to watch the world get born. To watch a writing creep from riverbed and river's tendril scratch the script on buried loam. The river and the city are together. One is the strip of silver mine where moon and water breed conspiracy of figures. One is figures when they're fertile, pictures when they picture more than someone meant. One is nurse for seedling gods, the water moon-rich white with gods not tapped; the other puts flesh on the godshape, hangs a race of different minerals above the moving facet. On the facets of air's diamond.

Happens once to bring the city from a cluster in the inner world to cluster on the surface. Happens twice once city's natal god is formed. Once first young triangles have learned their vine-coat and have taught themselves to stand. Then time for tape. Then turn for tape's regime of space, the air-tract hid between the glue and iron. Rooftop starts to push out subtle creepers. Bolt's charged skein of air has dome-shaped dreams. And the peaches ripe from sky at sun's dead hour meet peaches pushed through dead time of concrete.

Between the building and the dome, two copper vines have stretched. One up from pillared world. One down from sky that's learning pillars. Now they touch.

Now comes the fiercest god. From bowl of ink that was her womb.

¶

Box. Smallest unit of the city. Except when the city goes smaller. Flower of the streets; dark calyx where the street's outflow is held. Or lightened by a flood of crimescene red. Filled with mannequins exchanging their positions. Fatbrimmed hats drawn down over no eyes. Brims' stitching hides the stitching of an eye's black X, a reservoir for buttons, pearls, glass. Closed vision of the mannequins inside the red-drowned box. They wobble on their footless posts. They chatter in a spray of false chrysanthemums. Talking double, talking triple through the frills of plastic budding. Frills like the feeling edge of an anemone. A stringray. A living carpet of the ocean's meat. Boxes hold the coast of crimping flesh and guide it through the water. Boxes let their walls recoil and stretch. To feel the blind meat's flutter. A dark-eyed spot can grow and shrink to the feel the streetlight pointed inward. Can grow when moonshaft splits the box's border; can shrink when sun undoes the box and flattens everything away.

The street can only breed sometimes. Blood and blue slow water can't just come to it at will. If there is a will between them. And sun shows up a predator of streets.

Box camera. Tomb for long white gods. A place where skin goes sallow on its pegs. Ruffled wax that catches pinlight through the cave. The surface of a long white god is dangerous inside the camera box. It can melt to crests and eddies. It can pile into the fatty tongue of lava. It can slide away and off. Give its face to other racks of bones, give its beard unrooted to the sea. A box camera will make its god go missing. Don't look for it there. You'll be caught in a kneel and not have time to rise and turn. The shutter will slap down when you've just begun to bolt. Click.

Box spring. Anything that hides in soft protection. Anything gone teething when white walls enclose it. Anything made out of living coils that search for food inside your sleep. Anything that soaks up liquid dreaming. Anything that's stained with clipped dreams, their effusions. Rosewater, perfume, quick juice crushed from daisies. Handfuls of hissing grain. Handfuls of seed that clank and gnash. That tune your insects to their boxy clump. Anything that can control all insects from a distance. Any insect radio; any hex of wires that moves the grasshoppers to make a plague.

Boxwood. What takes the face of dead things. People freeze and strike on boxwood panels. Their softest parts – hair and eyes and bellyhold – each uncork a shiny tumour. Under varnish, they go crying. You can hear them when an uncarved person squeaks along the boxwood's finish. You can hear them in the curve that ricochets through rooms when someone rubs the boxwood into music. The residue of stories. Talking-oil that won't wash off the world.

Boy. Rag of danger. What's left alone in fields. What hums a dragonsong with no end. What steels the corn and grain with windy singing. A boy puts fragile whisper through your crops, if you have crops. They may have been blank and featureless before. But if you walk between their rows and feel a seizure coming, you'll know a boy has been stalking them. The boy is small and vibrates like a tuning fork. The boy can learn your speeches, slit them up the spine, and pull their skulls away still talking. The boy can stick a garbled syllable between two of yours and ruin the direction of your words. You will stand and gasp and grab your sides. You will feel your sight and smell and hearing moved behind yourself, and clamber back to wear them right again. The boy is singular. *Boys* is not the plural form, but another kind of animal entirely.

Boycott. Hands pumping up and down. Performed to wreck the sky in certain countries, at certain times. Almost always happening somewhere. A flash across dark lenses that reflects nothing. A chain of stolen burning that is blind to what gave off the light. A person's awful outline with no person at its centre.

Brace. The fastener of waters. Waves can pronounce the brace to lash themselves together. When blue-white pressure-lines still run between them, the water's made a brace. Enamel turning soft while toothpulp rattles from inside it. The bowl of teeth gone crooked when too much water hangs a shadow on it. The sheet of papery music woven by the teeth in that scenario. Foam and froth transmitted directly to your mouth. Skipped the sea, amputated from the unseen far-off crash, and wrapped around your jaw. For days afterward, you'll grind your teeth and hear nothing. Animals with more attentive hearing, like the dog and the boy, will drop to their joints and moan. You'll see the places where their meat is joined and know the brace is working. You can't undo the brace too early, or give it away. When your grinding makes a cool mist and the dogs no longer dip, the brace is gone. It will come at you again.

Bracelet. A metal vine that sleeps on human bodies. It enters as a gift. White arms between the long stone pools. Women rise from them in lengthless hours. Day and night abolished; silver radiance is patched dull on the walls. A bright shank of light filtered through some skin that deadens it. Women sit up from the waist and pause when their faces break the water's surface. If they have hair, the water draws a map between its strands. Small travellers could trace this map all the way back to women's brains. But so far no woman has remained in pools' quick breach for long enough. Which means that no traveller has been fast enough.

Or else those so fast have been too big; they've sat in soft stone chairs that line the women's poolhouse. They've watched brain-maps go to waste among the wavelets. And the smallest travellers have been so slow. They catch inside the ceiling and grow larger there like moths in chrysalis. Their slowness drags down into stopping, and wreaths of gummy rope restrain them in the walls. When the building is destroyed, they might be found again and taken for fossils. They'll be basically dead but still aware, the way that gods die. They'll huddle in the corner of a dusty star that fries them black when it explodes. Dust will gather in whatever corners of the building are left. Depending on how the building is destroyed, there may be more corners than ever. It may be parsed out to a chain of new corners. All the corner-worlds that slept inside its shape before. Laid out in a line between the waste-earth's slaggy horns.

Pause a pace to watch the mud go over us.
Pause and put your brow-steel toward the screech.

Hibou.

Woke and told no one.

No one there to tell. Woke and told no one except the me howled in the mirror. Flyblown glass with scurf of light across it; glass where darkfed me stands back of the glaze. No word or movement. Arm bent by no spineroot. Shoulders tightened back from no burnt wolfdog. Not the fly-eggs' garland on the glass. Not the broken sheen of solid mirror, the astronomy of jade-struck spit in starclouds. Not the dust that meditates new firing or the fire that shocks the stone god back to dust. So I woke and I told no one; and the me who has the mirror's shelter stood the way he stands.

Twist of rabies underneath his skin.

White foam sharp to draw off lips' curled shore.

The way he stands is white wood sprouting just beneath the face. The way he stands is marble meat that splits the waspwrack bark. The way he stands is blossom strangled by twinned vein, the flower that could feed the bee his molten stuff snuffed out by blood's quick map. The way he stands is undergrowth come forward: undergrowth bored through the warp of leaves. The way he stands is older stone, cool milk, the moon that sets to close to sun's dead boat – all this in pushing out of thirsty shell.

There's a Hibou in the mirror when I sleep. There's a Hibou in the mirror when another mirror bends to throw my bending. He shows me what I'll be when husk erodes. When river-finger picks the last dry strand and something old in me takes on my animal.

When the freeze has twitched by one degree and frozen marble turns to sluggish wet. Then the tree that hides it strains to hold the groaning artery.

Groan of wood pushed out beyond wood's orbit.

Groan of harp unplucked that stone still plays.

Then the channel bursts. The river bursts. The ocean snaps a brass-piled bank. And mirrored me reveals the secret juice. What shows when tree limbs take themselves for stars.

The Hibou in the mirror never walks.

But cities scroll along his flank; and every tree on every street is bursting.

Rain of milkstained splinters in his hair.

Pale.

A pale grey blank. The blankness always surfacing from corners balled with fire. Rose liquor built into a globe. Sun's purple come to know itself, the purple running vineshoot to the dirt, the dirt's rough arches gummed around with purple. Always coming out of this terrain. First inner eye of flower-sleep. First closed-eye vision of the winter hulks. What roots in eyelid's soil when wolf and wolf's quick train have shut down for the dying. Still you see the pattern of the skin. Where hide has taken scar, where wax left bald bolt through the wind-grained fur. Still the markings there compel a picture. No escaping map and map's sharp line. The crook holds rivers back; the dash and dash-gap ribbon through a field.

Still the alphabet and still the stained orange cave.

Still the woman peering from her shell. An abalone organ near the dark. Coins of cavelight breeding on the flute of living pearl. Still the woman plays at it. A carillon: a mass of bells with buttons at their feet. The button rings the bell; the bell-ring slashes soundplane through the failing plane of light; the cave's another organ with an organ locked inside. From the finger's whorl on ivory – the ivory sunk down by two-toned steps – the hammer like a nervous twitch – the resin-wood on chewed brass – and the ocean breaking soft through pitted harvest, breaking loud across the pitcrop on the metal.

Then the cave and woman make a bell around the bell.

Then the shoreline parts to air its rose. The coral rose in leaves of glass-veined pink. And on its crest, a rose; and roses to the cloudroof and the chamber of the sea, where coral needs no shape but its own tendril-wrack of gods.

Then I, who slept on sand, who felt it harden at my shuffle. I who knew that somewhere in the beach plate was a seam of frozen tremble. I who sounded for the secret line and heard the forecrack of its ruin. I who dug the sleeping place with nails now cut too short, so I could have the unborn rock along my skin. The rock now wet across its sleep between first rock and second. Or the hundredth and the hundred-first, the rock that never dies chained to its sibling lashed with blood. Copper blood's dried thunder on the second stone, the one where all stones tend. So I could farm the shellfruit and the cowry's trading husk.

But I couldn't live there.

Can't live there all the time. Can never fully leave it and will summon it tonight. Can never quiet stomach's pulse in days before the night-place. Can never cough the pearl and then be done. Still a rhythm gritted in my tubing; still a bow drawn on the face of my own reef. The sculpture stone I wrap my meat around is still beneath the bow of moving nights. And night sucks out an insect sound. Not cicada's cold electric screech. Not the hum of earthwires locked in locust. And not the cloud of flies in tune, the beecloud tightening up for chamber music. A different tone of bugs. A cricket stretched across the sea's dark bed and cricket's violin now long and low as horn of whales.

One cricket leg is belted on the world. And tide's the lacquered bow that comes to touch it. And far away enough, with lungs' low hearing, you can see the Earth sound jumping through weird soil. Blue dirt, green dirt, cloud of dirt's white ghost.

The planets are receivers for that tone.

And so am I. And so is everyone.

And Egypt is the city of receivers.

Except, I think, for me who stands in mirrors. Who gapes at something just behind my head. Who hides to match my turning and who gapes again when I've turned back around. The me who wobbles through a spit-stained womb. He is only pure reception and can't siphon off one sound. He's the one whose ankles break to catch the whole balled music, so he never catches anything. He's there now, to my left. I haven't looked. I won't look. Stem-juice murmurs through my neck, inclines it toward the sun that's mirrored West, but I will not look. I looked. I saw him rampant. Lions' sandstone through the peaks of pill-poor jars. Steady on the rolling plate of pills as I could never be on woman's sand.

I think he could.

I think he goes there, blank against blank sky, when sometimes I'm not crawling on the mirror. I think he holds grey glow on blank grey shore. Or puts grey path, a wilted onyx, through the cut of two grey hills.

I've seen that. It's the only time he moves. Breaks mirror's staring posture and leans toward the camera eye. Like searching it for something that's made blot. All the greed-drunk light behind the lens now stored like dead gods' stone. A magma chute. Now stored and now released: every vision hoarded through the glass. As he hoards my own dull sight at the mirror. And then rips away his own to match my turn. He bends toward camera eye to dowse the blot, the pearl, the ingot blasting red shafts through his blankness. All camera light gorged out, but at its lens-sucked strength. At the hollow shade where camera left it. Insect cask and casket of cut rice. All the backwash hoard without the chance to see it first; all light as seen through sandscratched shields of glass. All light the photograph that blanched and curled.

The photograph of mirrored me. His big-eyed face a half inch from the fire.

He knows that grey where day is flat against all flatness. Where the closeness of a whelk shell in the hand is still no closer than the tented sky. Where your face can chew another face but sky's wool shifts between them. I see him check the lens for jagged marks.

Then I see him jerk back, slow jerk sung with rippling clothes. Slow-motion spasm. And slow-motion makes him run. On heels at first. Then stumbling around to put his knee between the day's grey pillars. Stumbling where the columned air has set too hard. A copper glance, a second copper glance back toward the camera. I can see the penny-shine awaking in his eyes.

He's slowly disappearing.

I watch. And in the brain's valve used for watching, I don't notice that I've also disappeared.

Woke and told no one. But I saw:

Green sickness in the green tile wreck. This building is malaria's. Mosquito thrum along the blood. Sleeping sickness grouts the cracking wall. This building is a shrine to the disease god. To the god of glaze-eyed cow-deaths. Chickens matted bald and riot in their throat. The dog's limp leg in ruts of wheel-dug mud. Copper pipe is live with young mosquitoes; copper wiring breathes their livid eggs. I stretched my wragwrapped limbs on sea's green floor of tile. The failing squares combined in buckled plates. Continental drift where flyspeck breeds.

Alone now in the pale green ruin.

Now the ocean's shade a volley of clipped earth.

Now the ocean's shadow. Ghost of murdered god and of the young god never born. Ghost of brass-armed man along the river.

Woven when he likes among the treewarp. Appears when you've learned a math of leaves. When you come to know the hang of leafwrought music. Till then, all things are brass on brass. The murdered god will never surface from his mineral. Egypt is the river. As malaria and death-sleep climb the building's wrinkled rooftree, so this river is an Egypt in its course.

As fever-blossom routs the withered bulb. As useless sweat still pools a salty drip. As dwarf fruit splits its face on tile retainer. Green-glazed chop of clay downed now with webs of pulp. Apples browned to hives. Grapes become the crush of stagnant water. The vinestock dies of sucking fire. Not flame of ocean's face in grapeflesh, flame of yellow lynx-eye on the leaf. The sucking fire that bites wood from the bone. Takes cooking-smell away from tinder's grain. Rips secret meat from wood's all-hidden cavity. We don't know where it is, but we've all smelled it. The muscle gone to smoke when wood is lit.

You know the smell. You can't dig out its meat, but you know meat-smell from the warren piled with cypress.

This is what the dry fire kills. The fire of bleeding tubes and circle-mouths. The fire of animals like bags for blood. No facet and no face but washered mouth. No shape and no dimension but the sucking-hole. The leach-bag, tick-bag, bag of stolen harmonies. The blood is chord and tendril to your notes. The blood is low percussion when all other beating fades. The blood holds cymbal sheen and cannoned screech when nothing else has lip enough to keep them.

The dry fire draws to wood-blood. It wrenches out the flank and plane.

This building is malaria's.

And as dry fire scales up the building's heart – not its centre, but the actual iron heart –

So Egypt speeds across this river's loom. But one is a disease and one is Egypt. One's what killed me in my dream. Gunmetal to my temple. What held the gun to thumbs of killing men. The bug-suck in the tile.

The other one is Egypt. What is panther in the snowbank; what is ibis when the night falls through gold bricks. What holds the join between brass sky and river. What will watch when I look down to face the deep.

83

But all that later. Now the tile-green room. Its flush of toothless voices. Mangled from the intercom. They came with leather patches sewn across their mouths. They came with stitchwork bristling from their eyelids. Came with knees wrenched back to meet their wrists. Across that room, a mess of voices like a star's unhealthy birth. The sharp green knot above pale tile. The twist and strain of voice-nerves jumping out from nameless flesh. The body yet unformed. And pulling hard, too hard upon itself to take a shape. Always bulging meat that lashed and failed.

The voices spoke unwinnowed by their teeth. No tooth to fan the sound's wheat from its husk.

The voices came out tongueless. Tongueroot gurgles in the greasetrap of the throat. A rough-ripped clump of fibres rowing spit. The sound forever half the sound of drowning. Of voices caught between the final sea and brass-armed house beyond it. Always drowning, never fully drowned. The tongue beats broken eddies through a hurricane.

And then alone. The voices dead. And then know tile to be an ocean's ghost. Translucent shade of what once held up seas. This is emptied cask of seabed plates. This is belt that once conveyed the world. Now cracked on gurgle's crag, between dead voices. Saw the tile and knew it for its life. I'd scratched my finger on a bottlecap. Small meat of blood; but still it fed the room, still made tile speak. Caught the silhouette of shattered god, his music now a field of crack-hooked glass.

Then one clear voice:

"I who was wet am now the dead grasses' thousand miles.

"I grew in damp and milked the turning worm.

"I knew the phosphor locked in anglerfish, the sulphur hidden dark in vein-thin vents. I knew which chambers breathed and which were still.

"I did the coral's will.

"I split where coral seed charged up a splitting; and

"I broke where broken pearl threw out new roots; and then

"I let the worm's milk dribble to that brain. The pearl-lobe, rose-lobe, lobe of pink-blood coral. Fed them from the worm beneath all birth, the snake above all dying. From the ocean-tree locked in between them both. From the fruit that falls to know another hanging and that hangs to ripen softly toward the fall.

"I was wet. Am now a continent of broken pottery.

"I was wet and now am rattle of dead clay against the rocks.

"When vessel's smashed and talks with cricket-talk

"When vessel rubs its broken bow across a battered sail, a scrap of membrane,

"Rubs the bow along a veil that barely holds,

"A wind-strung clay that sun can hardly catch,

"I talk again. My talk is dry. But some will hear and hear inside it:

'I who am dead grasses' thousand miles – I once was wet.'"

Then clear voice stopped. Its thinness sprayed too wide.

So left the dead-tiled room.

And then went down a mile of stairs. Down past the zone where ocean's spine is raised. So that ...

Klang.

So that I saw her waking in a room strafed by incense. Brown impression of the brown world where she moves. Incense, oily bloom across her rafters' brighter face. Brown the tumbled brass behind white houses in a falling row; brown the lighter beams that crack against her if she falls. Brown the waking scar around her bark-scraped knee. Brown the tiny spears that fleck her iris blue. And buckskin fringing brown around her feet.

Her ankles brown where once she dreamt of rope.

Her papers brown, the newsprint that she glazes into chutes. The threadless maze of letters cut off to a prophecy. Dull sentence remade last words of the missing ancient storm. As MORE THAN EVER SUFFER. As TORNADO CLAIMS. As TALKED TO FOREIGN. Brown with print slid off the serif's feet, with *T* that slipped its scaffold.

The table varnished brown between black rivers of wet print. Black rivers where, in sleep, the owl will lead her to her bier. Move down them, back against the current, and a brown sheen lights the metal banks. Lights the sky whose edges droop with solder.

And still the girls' galleried faces shook me cold. Still the one girl's face, one eye big with chilled fever, fired out from the wall in repetitions. Every portrait smeared by gravitations toward one face, the same head sprouted from their stems of different daub. Still they shook my copse of barking reeds. The girl not her, the face not hers, the paintings hanged and planed by different hands. She lifts the window and one brownness crackles on another. Morning graphite smuggled on her nape.

Hibou.
And from that smear, the vengeful birds.
Now come the vengeful birds.
Birdstrike melted down. Back through the ear-whorl. Where bird's grain clots suspended. Hard water through the standing pipes of skulls. The clearing smell. The smell rips secret skin back to a seedbed. No more coat of time on waxy hairs. No more dirtweave gripping milkworn teeth. The poisoned gold comes forward from them. Back to metals from the metals tooth-ore sheathed. Like the iron man on seacoast. Iron lid sewn down by thread of iron breaker. Iron sinew through the needle's eye. Where cables groan the nightwatch. Where camels sniff the rust-flaked rings and burr.

Now the clearing alcohol.

Now glassmaker's vein within the rainwater. Barrelled ton shot through with pillars' burn. Now the maths divide themselves and water's little name is scattered. On one side the clutch of shrimp and waterbug. Of barnacle, of flat black shell with brain-root pressed into its members. The nervenap banded red between shell's leaves. You slit the walking tree in ocean's vault. You slit the standing tree where sky has just turned vaulted. You slit the bending tree that marries chamber-face to chamber and you drink the brassfed blood. Cymbals wheel within your pulse; the river watches.

Cymbals harden from the lap of shorecaught red. One tree gives meat, another fruit, another still the welded brazen seam. Brass and nickel clenched like murder's vine. And the river is their touch; and so can be their warp's destroyer.

Now the vengeful birds.

They storm a cloud in shallow water's diamond. See through the cracked green glasspane: something gathers. Whipped around the empty central cone. Ocean's path extracted now. One column's dented seafruit hangs between the sea-air's fold. And we bend from beach-sucked ankle. Dowse on pivot-bones that no longer pivot. The centipede's green augur shoves our balance. Legs bent along the rust of god-old rods. Now broken rust drops rustcoin through the lymph. Now lymph-store bulges sick beneath the skin. The old rod pushes; we incline or hide. We creak toward ocean's suture for the sight: a water column cut from wave on wave.

Valves of living shell now wrap themselves.

The water. Huddling grove for monster pearl.

The water: lung that twitches lung-wall's blackened digit. Coughs up the pearl now misted with my breathing. Coughs up the milk-blind orb made white with clipped breath's cataract.

The birds clump a darkness in the water. Before they sling bright arrows through my blood, they've got to barrel in the sea. Because their flock means searoof's gained another puncture. Birds don't come unless the second floor is shot. They lie sleeping in the ocean. They turn sleeping in the air. One breath is like another when no bonedrill bores them out. No disc of live white coral cut from either sky, the higher or the lower. So if I see the birdcone pull in blackness by its turn, I know. I know an instrument has punched through seafloor night. Will punch through day where day drops stone-fed milk from sky's grey sea.

It means the statue's woken up.

The seabed's furrow shortens. Buckles. Seizes.

The rows of seasoil mulled by patient worm – the rows contract. The mother worm is caught between their planes. Tail wrenched one direction while the head snaps in another. Now fat-leafed plants will feed on different dark. A compost made from halves of worms falls slowly toward the deep.

The trenches lose their sheet of new-laid scalp. Pink raw skin ripped back from jagged coast. The coast beneath the coast. One keeps water from the land. This, the lower, puts young rocks into the water. Rocks still wet and live as metal blood. All action mirrored. All acts of murdered day have brothers underneath the sea. We've seen it all. When blood of upper sun is siphoned into night, the low sun's blood clips up through sea-crack trench. Leaden ribbons laze through silent water. Or withered orbs that wait for sea to pop them. The ocean's riot lays its shape on Earth. The volume of the seabed organ, pipes full up with molten dust, gives form to newborn blood.

All in seizure's round. Called day. Called night.

And when the bird is vicious in my ear, those trenches shudder. Skin has grown since last disaster. Since last time the topworld fell and hidden sun kicked up the soft new god. Now skin peels back. Retracted like a tentacle to where the bird-cone turns. To where the bird-cone readies water's rise.

For me it means that soon I'll hear the swoop. That soon I'll cringe while bird-heat cracks me with its rays. That people walking under me will see the pale new twitch. The motion trapped inside time born too early. Day still premature. Still red where should be pink and grainless skin where sand should leave its whorl. Still fingerprint not stylus-etched in finger's waiting pad. But born already. Now plugged into steel that does its breathing, into plastic that can show it how to eat. Stitched to rubber folded like accordions. The tubing tree that mimes digestion. Model food through model guts, wall singed with model acid. A day that ought to be inside the root-brained tree until it's drunk the amber. But now ripping through the surface soil. Now howling tiny gales.

And they'll see me in that day. The people walking by. They'll watch when halfgrown future makes me twist and grunt and shake. They'll think it's my problem. But there's another movement in the birds that peck my eardrum. Other songs than those their chrome-cased beaks tattoo along my brain. See the metal filings pile up at my skullroot. See the spine's high knot go dull with flecks of beak-shaved lead. See the eye half-opened where a new cage hulks behind it. Can't do it now. A bird has wrecked the new machine in me. A bird has built the cagework city's spokes on nerve that roots my eye. Can only open it when crossbeams separate. Can only talk when cage lets go my tongue.

See that and think it all. But it's not.

All my dead machinery, return of shed birth-bones, is nothing to the statue stirring now beneath the sea.

Klang.

Ear for that machinery. The ear. So that he heard the pebble break for sea-limbs' rising. Heard the gravel's gap become a bone-map on the air. The yellowed gummy bone laid out in mudflat cracks. He heard the slats in tidal wall respond. The marrow's call now netted water, tubing through the deep. He heard the speaking tubes go out. The seafloor eye that rolls now. Sight to win his sightless eye. And lid to cover coil of years while his lid lets in nothing, nothing out. His own lid ragged now, the sea-eye is the gate that clips his vision. All light across his eyes dull sheen on nothing; so the light now black and whale's blood rope of purple. Light now intervals in alleyed dark. The phosphor traces fin-spot and the sodium marks ruck. A tiny cone that sections off the ocean. Puts a tower fifty miles below the world.

A rootclump punched through lowest seadark's crag. Now sap-balm tree that hangs toward inner sun; now lacquer sweat to keep away the dead. His own eye's fountain blank. His eye that takes no light now only giving. Where he walks, all the tree's crown hangs toward hell. And all the secret tunnel-flesh, the blind meat wrapped in grey, is motion of the first god's long digestion.

Sea's eye for his own.

One thousand years for sea to burst in pupils. One thousand years for sea-spine joints to make the eye's white turn. Rolls over when one copse of gods is dead. And rolls again to see the others worming, see the wormhoops stir on hell and start their crawl.

Some blind are blind when sea's live eye is shut. The socket breeds another seeing ghost: in music's strand, in foxes' blood, in sky carved up by hawks. In currents that the rockbird picks from lava's corpse. In currents of the blood's dead shift within the living mountain. Frozen gold and thirsty silver. The mountain's horn-capped lymph is there to sew; and some are blind in sewing years. Are tuned to hear the gold's soft beewhine cease. Are tuned to feel the star's quick ray that doesn't pierce their skulls. The sky a course of scalpel wheels – then not. Because all water breaks formation. Heaves and stops and starts to turn around.

No more brittle milk in jets of night. Which means no mountain's sluggish blood can hide. Which means the river's edge has come unstitched; and someone, Hibou, Klang, may slip the membrane's metal sleep. May put a hump in every bronze for bronze lumps singing radiant along his bronze-lace spine.

Any of these ways. And more. And always more than more. The petals on the seed, ungrasped in air, have always found their facet. Not all or even most blind catch the sea's eye. Some may catch but think it dead. A relic of cursed glass. Aborted planet. Still lodged in the living twin; reminder that each birth is death for millions dimmed unborn.

But he had sea-piped ears. Had brain's maze zoned with breathing coral. And the sea eye for his own, the eye that opened at his birth. Looked up through the water's heaven. Felt a cylinder of loose-bound reeds cut through the ocean fold and touch its iris. Felt the pupil gape to let in needles dropped from star. Their edges blunted by the time, the black, the water. Now only seeing-rays. But some days drills; and some days, trepan for the spongethick skull, the skull too walled with chambers. Some days, cup where bone dies quickly. Where the citrus bite of skull-cell leaks and brain's sharp bees escape.

Day that ends with one tree haloed. Burst of golden bees now set in bark. Cross the sea of moving leaves to reach that tree; and young god, god made young to stay that way, picks ant and tooth from compost for the weaving of his wreath.

Ear for it. Where other wreath was welded from the speartips at a gate that now guards nothing. Where the rubble's foot has dug through death-rich loam and come to tap the rockshelf.

And so:

Went down. Dead nerves now looped around the place we left. Dead man whose nerve-thread got pulled hard. A file of empty rope piles. Baskets yet unburnished into life. We went down and saw the woman back of us begin her weaving. Hanging nerves on any faucet of the island that would wet them into life. Some from the dormant hives to suck a honeyed current. Some across the windows so that day would charge their coating, force their sheath to wind against its burn. And some where we went down, the path to ocean's edge, to meet their sibling wires in seaboard mud. The ivy tendril of the city that comes up from marbled sea.

But rarely, rarely seen. In constant motion. Turbine red and ivory drives vein-sight through the Earth. The spider under every city branches off his web. Extends the hollow zone, the place where goats and sheep get lost, out to new city's pearl-laid brain. That's always. But it's rare to watch the spinning. Watch the spider at its work of giving time a shape. Of marrow wound across the jade face of the deep.

And now behind us, where the woman spun. A yarn of nerves that followed us to seaside. Nudged around the boat and sniffed the slat-edge furred with salt. I looked at him and he looked back at me. Nothing to do. If city would crash up through boat's frail belly, then it would. If city would embalm the boat, a diamond cyst to work its heart against, it would. The city does. We watch and do and we can learn to plumb the city's heaven. But not then. The nerve let go the boat and slithered back. Now water on its tip; now shape of seagod in the eye behind the eye. Where nerve would curl and rest, the eye called city would see coral god on vision's edge and wonder at the phantom. Would see shade of seagod dimly in the dim scope of the skull and wonder why. We saw it start. I looked at him. He looked at me. With both had eyes cropped out with holy ghosts like cave-roof hackles teeth.

3rd.

She dances, white foot white where dance is mayhem. In the silver jangle spoked to tambourine. Inside the grape's dim riot on its vine. The broken dust turns deep when white feet sift it. Learns the tidepool shape, the water-suck like bands of ancient rock. And then a blue pump through the beast; and then a new rock's generation comes to crown piled strata. Poison-vivid blue that bombs away what paler blue has spent forever seeing. Spent the cities' chain, the link of Egypt from the first time it went under.

Time doesn't begin when firstborn Egypt mounts its sphere. Time begins when firstborn Egypt lets the wind pluck rubble's harp. And all Egyptians have exploded into fossils.

She dances. Border-feet inscribe the line of wolves. What any Egypt's city forces up by forcing down. The pressure of the steel-ribbed glass and glass that cautions steel. Always brunt of building's posture sizzles through the Earth. Always toward the lowest ocean. River of the livid inner sun; river of the metal gods from whom all cities grow. And cities' sinking kicks up hidden cyst. The tumour worshipped and forgotten. Bone deformed in birthsac that was prophet while it moved, that, dead, predicts a virus through the corn. The city seeks the river; city bleeds away without it. So the bronze walls form. The cup and bowl that house Egyptian theatre. The phantom fan that stitches Egypt's sound with trails of melted light.

She dances out the wolf-drum. And her dance gives birth to inky scar across the sleep of moles. Puts clotted ribbon in the limeseed, raises walls of knife-fine fear that make the birdflight loop. A hawk is basin bent around her updraft. Dog is what she black-chalks on the wind. A scrape of coal sees white and black from coal-gripped seashell eyes. The shrimp falls dazed from paper skin; the whelk leaves off its shell to pleach with coral.

Place expelled from place. The site that cannot hold to placement. Always chrome derangement through the night. Then always coat of rotting scales. A reef of shingled skin that seeps like bee-dance. Toward the crux of blank coordinate. Toward the thing that only Border knows as thing. And Border is no gentler to her own. The trashpiles brim with women's mangled husks. They dip and hang from knobs of junk. They make an icon for clay shards to ring around.

They freeze an alabaster vein on blue-green upsurge from the deep.

A burning-ground is ocean's highest shoulder. Every morning, it holds up a few more broken women. Or Border shunts them up from ocean vents to shed in rasping air. Or else does both; and there are murdered women locked between the vertebrae of sea. Who wave like weeds when wave-crest blows a hanging scab from sisters on the surface.

Siblings. Like the sea that carries whalebone to the sea that carries hawk.

Hibou.

For too long now I've dreamt a locust murder. A dream has been the roll of one peaked rind onto the next. And behind the rank of seats, behind the six or seven words that dreaming kneads into my jaw, I've heard the crest and thump of brass-shelled wings. I've heard the desert rattling inside those words when speaking turned to gum between my teeth. Gurgling *tar, tyro, Tyrol* while my palate's rubber hummed with goldsoaked catacombs. And in every hole where gold blew out the slosh of rubber tongues, a locust smacking screen doors; a locust sputter underneath the lamps. Sound of fingernails on white tape. Sound of dry leaves harpstroked by a scarecrow's rake of fingers.

Klang.

And then went down.

Set hard to keep away the gloaming dead. Though sun alive, though twilight not yet fallen. Still the dead were sharp again. As when the blood has wet their hackled throats. Set hard though I was moving. In the vessel on the arteries of Egypt. Cask of speed that buzzed me with its workings. Bright machine within the torso. Felt my own machinery respond. Though set as hard as I could make it. Chest's twinned owls call up the coughing fluid. Jaundice eye calls hoot to jaundice eye across the empties of my breastbone. Heard the insects of the air root through dark leaves. Heard the dark heat rise from pit of heaving tigers. Heard that somewhere was a house borne high on earth by bone-post fences; but that I wasn't in the house nor gave the bones to mount its picket. Heard the milk that men aren't meant to drink. Heard the toothworn nozzle wriggle from its sheath.

Here inside the curve of speed's thick shell. Can draw the hollow knock from knuckle on its lining; touch the inner skins, the inner worms that grind away in coils. Here inside the shell that speed secretes when I go down among the obelisk and tower. When I try to hum for language of the dead. Until I hit the pitch that makes them vibrate in their husks. A dead milk-eye shaken from cornsilk charred by fall.

And then went down. The snakes still grappling in my head. Whelped slick in nighttime when I cowered through red light. When there was only one red room, all loud with glances, and the street beyond it mothering new devil. Muted blare of phosphor off the city's lettering. And I still carried basin of the snakefight. Through a row of pyramids. Gave onto darkness feathered out with hissing wheat. Still had the snakes to write a knot-book in my heavy skull and felt when pyramid droned them alight.

I didn't know if they were given to strange gods. I didn't know if several gods were buried in them, slowly blooming stars to pump the pyramid's gold blood.

But when I passed a certain one, left snake lit up its brand of teeth. The new book scorched across my brain. Most likely old book, first incised through city's roots and now resurgent. Old book forced through plies of oil by city's weight. The book that built first boundary stones, killed victims so their juice could speed first temple. Book that screamed on crude young altar. Book that first contaminated fur of trees: a vicious thing in moss. A spot in flies' eggs. Skin-trapped eye beneath the outer skin of lizards, seeing only matted cross of flesh's press, but open. Always open. Not put out because a secret. Looked like dapple on the green. Looked like bulb of fruit to pilot lizard's nervous atoms. The young eye of the book soon come to burst.

A spray of weird new tears shoots geyser out of newt's torn spine.

And then the book's old ivory torn up to wheel for columns. Turned and turned until the Earth's deep text falls off and has to live through smaller needles. Then the crumbling and the raid. Then the faces painted so that murder comes in butterflies. Then the man asleep whose face will knit to ledge of seaweed's rock. Whose sleep marks out the lifetime of his race. When it began, the ache tattooed between their hungers. When it ends, neglected gods will let their animals run free.

An Egypt split while huge white hounds run up the pyramids.

An Egypt split because the parrot's beak sucks honey from the sacrificial pit.

An Egypt split because two moths have put the cancer in two pillars.

And old book grips itself in secret hollows. Old book sprouts a war of faces. Teeth beneath the thin meat at the armpit. Empty pouch of eyes strained up against the weak rear knee. Every open place begets a tongue. Every orifice lets out a slow tarantula. Each one an Egypt.

And then went down. Watched the girders flash above my head. Watch the other shells drive soundless toward the hell-mouth. Down beneath the present Egypt, lower even than the Egypt come before it. Down where every Egypt ends when river sifts it. When the flood that writes all things has marked a blank space through Earth's strata and the city's beaten powder filters down. Long reflex of the city's opened rose. Came up from river. River claims it. Even if we kill the flood and salt its bed. Beneath it river plate will still conspire.

Went down there among the hardened fragments. Gallery of fossils. Out of sequence now. But form another sequence. Broken star-belt drifts but soon enough responds to new star's suck. Now the shards of Egypt lose their siblings but cohere in new dead flowers. Can see among them what has lived in secret through the whole long roil of cities. Dog-god made of mirrored black stone mimes city shape. One dog-god squat with buttered fat. Another like a calyx made of needles. Another broad in barrelled chest but set on tiny legs; another like a child at top but mounted on a pair of lobster claws. All lean out from sconces in the rock. And all their satin blackveins breathing cloud. The swarm of radio dust whose sound turns solid, grasps itself to make a dim new sun.

Sun-chamber in the gallery of fossils. All born here. Mostly die. But one dies constant, drains into the night. And one more is the brain that's wrapped in Earth, that dreams in shaky hieroglyph; then river reads the scarab script and unborn city quivers in its root.

¶

Wine. Middle press of water. What the riptides feather. What squeezes out of anything that's known the ocean's pressure long enough. When the Earth berserks a final hurricane and octopuses thud in empty canyons, there is wine. The turning eye, whitewater in tattoos around it, has a jellied sugar wine around its pupil.

Wing. The most powerful. Sometimes. A tent made out of little splintered trees. A metal scythe that cups the smallest current. Wings are instruments for sounding out the air. In day they find the lines, the curls, the tumours. Veins that barely stay beneath day's skin. Arteries all tickfat and at every beat a threat to day's white temples. Scabby, strained. Too old too soon. Bleached and dried by cataracts of sons. Daughters blow across them in a zephyr made of sand. Underneath the temples roll two horns in dreaming. The wing can dot their outlines. Slap day out of its husk and prompt the day's horns to emerge.

At night the wing is motionless. Because the night is empty – of day's mist and powder, of the sunshaft and the sunface – the wing doesn't need to beat. It can ride the music that's obscure in daytime. It can glide through dark trees and fix a lamp inside them. The winglight leaved to circles in a nightdark tree is one real form of god. These gods will mostly leave you alone. But it's a bad idea to irritate them. You stand at middle distance and watch bees' small golden cities rise between the leaves. You watch the hive sprout bridges, girders, crossbars. You pay attention to the river god, a flank of yellow glowing where the wing cleaves from its tree. You notice how the river god is moving under hive-cells. Moving in the buildings that they brook.

It's important to be quiet here. If you try to speak, your alphabet will sew itself to wingbeats. Consonant for feather thrashing feather; vowel for hanging flight that smooths the feathers down. Don't talk. The tree, the wing, the river bees can hear you. And one of you will have to be a plague. When hearing is the question, one of you will have to ride a plague-bout over all the others. Either you, a stomping piston through the bees' warm reservoir. A row of punching pins. Pneumatic hammers that drill out the honey vessel. Or they, a race of metal stars that pings your city into panic.

Insect bodies thumping off a corrugated wall.

Wink. Sleep that didn't catch. Invitation to rip into someone else's sleep. Act of awful danger that can only be committed by someone who didn't mean to. Didn't mean to make the wink, or didn't mean to know what winks can harbour. The wink sends out a portal into sleep-seas of the winker. It jerks across the room like sonar. Batsqueak rolled in wheat and mud and gravel. Until the scurf is large enough to force the squeak into a kernel. Kernel: an unborn thing that waits out years before its birth inside a gritty envelope. Any thing unborn, and any safety gnashed around it. The kernel is a secret or a legend; legends are like secrets, but instead of turning blank to hide themselves, they shelter in disguise.

The legend puts a shock of dryness in the old man's voice. It makes the fire flare browner. A pad of sugared gel inside a rock that old men find along the beach. A hanged wolf with a broken neck that drums dull wolf percussion on a treetrunk. These are forms of winking when the wink rolls like a legend.

If someone winks at you, be careful. Act like it's not important, or even maybe charming. But quickly catch your own eyes in their turning. Bend toward the wall and quickly blink. You may want to laugh quietly to satisfy the winker. A loose wink, one that grafted onto no one, is a terrible and silent bird. So catch the wink and let it start to set. But scrub it all away by turning, blinking, laughing.

If a vagrant wink sticks to another person, there will be a tunnelworks of sleep that night. Transmitter and receiver will bob and cough at distant ends of one meat cord. Like an umbilical cord, but with its suckers planted on the winking eye. An anemone as long and thin as fear. And poisoned hairs arrayed to buzz along a sleeping eye's dark frame.

Winning post. Hard to say. Where people sweat and smile above the faultline. Where someone right now shakes a stranger's hand. And just beyond them, underneath their cliff, the earthplates smash together noiselessly. The world comes out in jagged bricks like bad teeth. To mark a belt of crushing that ignores the winning post. To score the sky with rare clinking, so later skies can be torn away more simply.

Winnow. The smallest thing. The act of holding. The act of seeing. The act of eating. Maybe acts in general. Maybe the act of having words for anything. The act of having faces in the darkness. The act of showing fireglow on the curvature of skin. The act of cutting with a tiny shriek. The act of grasshoppers who bow themselves. The act of violins whose notes end with a drip of milk.

The act of turning grain into a constellation. And sleeping underneath it for the night. Letting grainpests, lice and locusts, pick over the stars.

Winter. Habit of the Earth. A way to show its horns and plated skin. At certain times the Earth needs dark to pool inside it. There's a work that it can only do in darkness. So it bristles up a race of statues. Patchwork animals in granite. Animals forgotten, unrecorded. Or yet to be. Animals that stalk the seafront when a day is only pink and orangey tendrils. Vines that sting the ocean with a bright juice. When a day is only pulp and rinds, and night can chew them down into a paste. The daystung ocean glitters but won't move. The night will move it through a silver medium. Record the ghost of moving on its silver skin, and watch a surge of ghosts until there's day again.

Or not these animals. Or these animals, but also others. Nearer to the water. Just between the shoreline and the seabed. Posed on pedestals and waiting for the arm that rips the ocean from its pegs. Waiting for the sound of cracking shells from high above the night. The sound that tells them: race over the world. Because there's not much time.

Hibou.

There have been other Egypts. More than tooth that plants the nerveroot. Wild black grain. The black wind wild above it; and in black earth, nerve's coil slips the planted tooth. Other Egypts. With them, other music. If they'll found the newest city, draw the marble reeds from where they turn the shore, they'll have to separate those musics. All the shaken sound of bronze in discs. And all the skin on skin, the palmline married palmline in black air above burnt eyes. They'll have to winnow out the sound. Pluck newborn monsters from their birth-pods on the vine.

Voice came to me and said, *To sort out the animals.*

Voice said, *What looks on stalk-eyes through the gunhole in the tower is not what looks on stalk-eye where the sea's spine sews its bite.*

And time is what we call the chain of Egypts. Word whose tap and gum wrap over Egypt's plated links. In fields that bear the city, where I take my sleep and waking, there are chainlinks blinking gold from row-massed wheat. I carve the night by sounding wheat's brass corridor. A hallway turned to black when Heaven, live in metals, turns the living metal dead with fertile deadness. Another Egypt wrote: *The Heaven has eight ways to summon black; there are eight blacknesses inside it; and the eight directions, named to splice the rose, can all turn black when Heaven takes the metal to its house of death.* If there will be another Egypt – time will keep the turbine sharp and hidden – it'll have to learn all breeds of black. Will have to listen when the ghost and ghost are planted by the dead house, asking after Egypts long since thrashed to dust. Long since alive in living metal, dead by gold's dead turn between the days. Long since pressed and cut by steamshaft into coins that rest the sea.

And long since filings' dust. The rose that crowns the cave of wavered gas. Of dead strands in the air that shape dead vision.

The rose on magnet's crown to meet the rose that coral's engine pushes into taut-stretched night.

So the other Egypts come. By one or many. In their wholes or in an arm-copse grafted to another's trunk. In eyes inked red on waving flesh-poor hands; in kneecaps ground to fill the pigment's tray; in hanks of dry black hair that toss in dryer blacker wind to show me how the sea-snail's toss is formed. The other Egypts come through women's eyes. Through light that slits the dark's quick grid and comes from nowhere I can see. Through women's light thrust up through fine black mesh when night should damp them. In muscle curled around the absent bone. In marrow that no more respects the bone-wall's claim and leaves like bloody moss. In vagrant oysters of the ear, now split from skull-stitch, crawling slow. In scalps that hang from waving wire, that stop the wind against their sticky sides and print a muffled music on the fields. In one sharp bow drawn through another's strings; in strings like cone of spears that howl a hornet's mating touched by foreign bow. The Egypts do not always come entire. Come in a forehead gnarled by surplus eyes. Come in a spine re-welded so that spineheld animal, what used to be a man, can sit in humps and breath the vision's lethal gas.

In woman clothed with tatters, wasted hall behind her, crying something that the frozen scene keeps mute.

In man who freezes calm when gentle sphinx crawls up his legs and waist and belly. Looks for answer of himself within the man-eyes; looks to hear sung out the only man that walks in day's three ways. The only man for sphinx's alphabet. Can't draw him once, in one position. Fan of men: at left a crawl of burning fat, at centre upright jackal, and at right the three-legged scratching in the sand.

The iron man I visit by his coast is propped on pillar.

The Egypt rising now is scorch of fats.

So I, and ocean's rose above, are jackals shorn of crouch.

Are goldplate crocus-needle toward the spring.

Today there rises Egypt of dry seeds. Today the god is dry and full of seedpods, and the rhythm is his crack against the breeze. An air in blocks. An air of bellied canvas. Pregnant linen under cloud of swollen haunch. The god is dry but never empty. What was birthing nectar is the food of secret birth. No syrup on the seed; but still it moves. And cloud has rolled down scale of blue-shot grey, has brought the untouched ocean down to kiss the touched. Has thought the god gone dry was vacant in his husk. A flap of cornsilk holed by wind-rot. Flap of chaff that dryness fused. They meet in water, latent sea that strikes from glassy chamber; when the water goes, their meeting sews its horn. The sutured burr curled through a hairpatch.

So now the Egypt dries and sphinx shakes dryness halfway up god's chest. But the dry beast comes to surface in a spray of upraised hands.

First the patterned shiver. First the field of withered grain, the shaking field where sister-shake stands out. And then a lump of lava sound. The mirror's black sucked through volcano teeth. What mounts the river-sun on ridge of old suns' death is clutched and calmed. And the black rock, hard as ripped-out teeth that turn in pregnant soil, comes through a narrow gate. Comes hissing through the grates of cooling death. We suck it out with hollow reeds; we wait till reed has lost the killing heat; we shave the wood away with thumb-whet knives – and there a mirrored column glints its black. This first of all the Egypts that today will charge with speech.

The day is length of Egypt. Stood in regiment to talk when night goes clear. When night is acid with a dried-out headache smell and laps the cornered pool of day from oil's last cornered sac.

A luxury of vipers. Snake-bloom moves; and with its movement comes the hand. The viper's nest has cooled to match the mirror. The mirror is snake-lined, gives back glint of viper jewels and fang. We've stripped the reed and found the black proposal. We've accepted it. I haven't and you haven't. But the We of other Egypts talks with one voice out of seven empty mouths. And nine, thirteen, and twenty. The We here hulks to mime a solid beast. No word from beast-bright tongue, now hard at root with dreg of undrunk blood. No word before the language comes to Egypt. When the alphabet is scratched to sound the god: his depth and width, the ships that pass or founder.

The We has not yet found the word. But it doesn't matter now.

Old Egypts pass above, hang to the saggy roof of cloud.

And the crowd's another animal. Permission in its shape. That crowd is present means: We have accepted. We are here to fathom magnets in the marrow; we are here to touch the lodestone blasted fathom-deep by shots of warring suns. We are here to catch what orbits in the catching-belt between high sun, the daystar, and low sun of tendril's drink. We are here to free the dog that takes its hackle from our border. We are here to loose the battery of lynxes.

We are here to be the iron car and iron cats that pull it. Where the voice-scrap hangs in alley shook by bombs, we feed on scraps. Where the warning tower crumbles from its goose-eye, we link arms around the base and lift our dusty lips. To slip the noose from man to man. To make the god that hangs with one knee riveted to next.

Too late by now. Once "we" escapes from crowd's still-rolling lip. Not the lip creased on dim faces. But the mob-edge bent like seaweed in a shallow cup of jade. The edge of people's mass. The burning zero of a body that our bodies leave behind.

So now the mirror. Now the soilstuck teeth.

Put one hand up to signal our permission. Right arm straight. All palms face toward the morning zone. Where sun is captain after bleeders' night. Strong with the juice again. His pink bags full of red, his red hall spiced with plated white. Now the sun is bark around a cluster. Now the cortex of a shield, the safety wood. Renew the current hopped from lymph to bulge of lymph. All things, not less the sun, are fragile sheath around an island chain. Peninsula of furnace and a laurelled dynamo. All things, not less the sun, are all things. The crowd of men is buffalo. The buffalo is tent and meat and city. And the city is a gear-stitched bird with beak on copper hinges; and the bird sits heavy by an iron shore run through with wind's wild crack. And watches us, the crowd. And watches Egypt.

Old iron man, when blood has wet his voice, will say: *All things are lights.*

He'll etch a tag to give his word dimension. It's in an alphabet that I can't read. Looks like: *kuthera deina.* But strange god is in their aspect. And strange god has come before as seeming letters, in the shelter of a crossbarred H. Coiled slick within the hollow of a *d.*

All palms toward site of sunbirth. So all backs toward sun's white morning. So all nape-nerves, gilded lifeknots cresting spine, are turned away. Toward night that needles ivory from reddish marbled day. And the right hand up. Begin the dowsing sway. Crowd's bodies briefly separate to grope for each one's cog. Brass fingers on the hipjoint. Kneading flesh for gear's teeth. Kneading crumpled skin, now harnessed to a furred elastic wave. The gyroscope is there. The fingers won't discover it. That's part of this old Egypt. Have to search to start your dancing; but the dance arrives while search is dull and ache. Can't pick its prickled tuft from off yourself. It comes apart. It comes to mock the search.

Belly's bowl is brimmed with sluggish gold. With wine whose silver jumped the milling red. With flesh of flesh, the brown sheath on the muscle's vampire pink. Belly's bowl is dormant, and the pelvic bowl below has slipped its grind. Other Egypts come to build the new one. And each one is script that reads you off a song: *there are two rivers in your basin. There are as many rivers there as fonts of blood. There are as many veins as siphon from the river; or as many as the riverbank will hold in Egypt's youth.* The capillary gains your pelvic mound. The river's mouth is sucking on a tree that drops young worlds as red-ripe fruit. Still hot from broken pools. The factory of rocks beneath the rock of ocean's scar.

Your belly is a warehouse now. Your chamber underneath it, life of unborn squids, the life that falls from skyroot tree. The coral god rolls frigid seafloor eye. Rolls up and back on phosphor plain's abyss. He knows the flower and the pad. He knows the fan whose fibre seethes with pulpy birth, the tube whose walls forgive an unknown passing fish. How many shrimp before the tree? How many crabs and fins and nameless gill-necked things?

Or more: how many cherry stones?

That meditate how many stone-brain cherries?

All Egypt doesn't lap this bowl's quick brim. It isn't all the Egypts, nor is it all of any one. Other bowls have poured their sibling oil. Other bowls have given floor to where the threshing steals off purple dye. The alphabet and god are not all here. The flat black eye with black vine crosswise on its face is still a dream. But still it can't be left out of the building. Still the city has a vault between its hips where monsters first put crooked backs to soil. And still the root of ivy's clasp turns ringlets on their feet.

The meatless bones have shed their sulphur now. Crippled cricket borrows pelvis for its bow.

Klang.

Down the ladder. Down where had been up.

I climbed to shove away the haunt of waters. Sea had turned me on its edge. Sea had picked me where it splices with the sky. I saw the air's wild fingers shaken with invading foam. Creeping oil with seablood on its film. The foam caught stone-shape from the sky's interior; beaded it along the ocean's roof. And sea pulled down the rooftree from its corner. The ocean folded. Lined with messy lengths. My boat fell in a crease of new-mapped blue.

Sea had me on its row of teeth. The ocean-spine where surge takes grey hard points. When the trunk that held four oceans flat was shivered at its root, the silent squares of water slipped beneath me. I heard stone glint like silver fish. Heard pebbles scurry down the seawall and take shelter in their hives. My eyes were seafoam-blind, but sound lit up my seeing. Heard the little rocks report to little rivers; heard the riverbeds that dry out in the ocean's shade. Heard old rivers tremor to the old forgotten gush. Ancient water where the only wet was memory. Newborn water's course: a blast to shake remembered bite. Their walls. Like tubes or incut Vs. Like toothless mouth worn square. Like delta flats that lisp with woven mud.

New tide set off explosions when the ocean turned. And I, hanged from its pointed edge; I who broke my back atop its wall – I saw the snakewet whistle through the rocks.

Where water hadn't been: now tide. Now tide's dark rip.

Where river was a fish-old sign. The crab-legs, bug antenna, whisker prod. The clean young bugs that clambered in its rubble. Where river was a shape pressed into walls – and when other people hid there, under earthen roof, they wondered if the water really flowed. They saw the flood's insignia and said: Here was a face. Here was ripcurled beard and hand with heavy weapons. Here someone rode the dolphin's length; here another blinked beneath the weeds. They said: Here dryness was a scar. Here the people wavered under dry tattoos. They said: Could you recall that shape of eyes? Could I recall the stretching lens, the envelope gone slack to see those floods?

They had questions. They didn't have a memory. Not of that; but they remembered other things and put the fish, the water in that mould. The grain and warp. A mud-boned skeleton impressed the cavewall. It was a rattled animal they'd never seen. They said: Must be an animal. What animal could it be like? Could I recall the fish before the dawn?

Could I see layered shallows when no sun picks out their number?

Could I see the fish bent ply-on-ply and take no guess at how they bended in the day?

Here three prongs split ocean's canopy. Here a black-eyed diamond built the walls. Here a daughter struggled from a shell. Here were men whose necks went red with fur. Here were tawny shoulders over legs' clean piston. Here were owls that wrote and trees that read their carving. Here the bubbles lit a hissing beard. Here white meat held firm with wrinkled glass: three bands of meat inside the circled shaft. Here muscle turned at intervals. Here man lost its old green sheath. Here men's arms bulged through the plant-wall and their fingers stretched to snap the vegetable web. Here the root and bloom and minor leaf was rolled up in his spine. Here the secret plant became his brain. Here his skull began to glow with candled reeds. All true. All true.

But that's not all. The flood returns.

The chimes that flash in pebble-glint sound live again. The harp sewn into moving air plays spider-chord. The flood returns: cracked river's thousand arms restring the harp.

The flood returns beneath its basin-wall. The thousand arms of cave-fish wave from under ocean's glass. They're silent. But there's wavetalk in the splash. Seagod limbs are wheeling in the furnace. Domed fire that cools in glass. They can talk other ways than this; can talk in almost any way; there's hardly any talk that doesn't feel their turbines whirl. But now it's time for seagod's quiet talk. His lapping sentence. And the tributary spider writes it down. He says:

I cracked the riverglass.

I made the breakwork hum with fluid.

I kneaded glass to ocean's bone; when it was running-hot, I let it run.

When crayfish typed the fields, I passed a fertile water under them.

When lobster flared, I named the trenches in his fan.

When octopus was green, I shocked the shoreline with his blue.

Seagod talks. His voice of worlds is hammered to the world-screen. And I was on the ladder then, gone down. I had gone up. But down replaced me. Seagod's voice thrummed muffled into quiet ocean's pouch; but it rose up through the shore and tuned a tree of falling clicks. I fell and heard its fall. I fell and saw the rockslide, saw the pebbles climbing down to make the seagod's hammer strike. A tiny instrument. Thin finger on the world's eardrum, tapping rhythm come undrowned. Thin brass pan that took the tap as marking. As scratched residue of wings; as fins that waved through goldlight so the ocean would know that here a wing had passed.

Here was one flower of bones. Now another calyx swarms in sheets. The bone's gone out of it. The bone-stem is a branch of veins on fin's transparent paper.

I fell. The small new flood recalled its size. I fell toward it and it got bigger. Maybe one and maybe both. I can't say now. Not important. What's important is –

I fell through water-time and scratched the tunnel wall's descent. Fell so far that rivers grew where rock remembered them.

I'd climbed because the wall had promised coils. Dripped me down a snakebraid – lock of oil, a twine where amber caught itself. Something laid atop it in a pile. I climbed the wall to find out what was braided. Saw loops of hair impressed on soft stone walls and firelight of dead gold around them. Saw awful drinks that poured too slow, black sugar's gleam, a continent of tar. Saw grape branches pricking through the water. Grape skeleton that breathed into my nose and made me flinch.

I saw the cup tilt over and nothing pour out. But the cup wasn't empty. Filled with sweetened press-blood of the bushes. Gummed fluid stuck to its own surface. I saw a killing lake that glaze had stunned, and I had to drink it. Something on the wall was slipped in coils and pounded into sandstone with the coil-weight. It's not my fault. I knew. It's not his fault.

Klang doubled on his boat's bent floor. The salt-cracked staves uneven. Scurf of shrimp music in the salt's dried spray. Feet moved low by night so they wouldn't upset the boat; feet scuffled over wooden warp to keep the boatmoon steady. The moon touched down along the tide and rolled: one crater held the centre, and the pockmarked moon revolved around that dent. Night's stiff white hair was turning on the soft white disk.

Klang slumped in the boat's curve and wondered at the moon. If it had been too long since eating, sleeping, seeing flesh. If Klang's moon was the moon brought down from night-mount or if lesser moons, the orbit-birds that flock where moon will be, had found him. Albino bats that flutter through a gravity like milk. If this one were the first, a crashing train of moonbirds had to follow. His boat would roll and snap while blind wings of the moon made everything go hollow. Scooped the ocean out and carved its standing water walls into a corridor. Scooped Klang out of his place, an old man nightdrunk in a boat, and made him touch the kissing sand of seafloor. Made him walk the waters' hall. A triangle slashed down through the ocean height with Klang moving tired through the bottom. Looking at the whale-shape shadowed in the wall. The fans of red-green sea flesh breathing ocean-wall's quick glass. Klang looking at the metal pipes that groan and rasp their choir through the underworld; Klang looking at the squid turned into statue and the octopus that drains its ink to match the falling moon.

White nubbed flesh that slaps against the sea's clear lava.

Klang to hear its slap and cower. Klang to palm the rippled wall and sound it for a break, a crush, a hairline crack. And not to take surprise when his hand slips through the standing water's grain; and not to be surprised enough when ocean meat, an octopus that pumps inside the wall, trails a pointed finger on Klang's wrist.

Could he feel the separate ply of flesh beneath the wetness?

Could he have a hand in water's diamond tower and know when he had touched the thing beneath the damp?

He feels the tentacle slip lightly on his wristbone. And he thinks he feels the water between them meet, compress, flow out. He thinks he feels the ocean gape to give their touch admission. Sea's last fibre broken so a bumpy point can rifle through his arm-hair.

He thinks about that. Then, too late, he whips his arm away and thinks: Oh god, an octopus. Scratches his wet wrist on salt-tough pants. Jewels of salt, new wetted after drying months, go clipping through the ribs of ocean's floor.

The moon landed in his boat; the sea piled up in walls and Klang walked its damp hallway, stumbling on the sea-bone knobs. That was last night. A night however many years ago, or when Klang was already long past old. But maybe a different old. Maybe an old through which he had to dive down fathoms and spring out young again. The Klang who lies here, drying in the thick wind on his bed, is not the Klang who felt soft moon-edge tilt a rotting ship. They have been the same and stood back to back.

They've stood front to front and traded air. Breathed into each other's mouths and noses, so they'd learn what parasites moved in their lungs. Learn what one Klang reaped between the sickles of his throat and if it killed another Klang to try to breathe it.

They learned how each one hollowed out the air and stole its juice. Gave back an air-husk ready for the plants. They found that they breathed very much, but not exactly, alike. One man felt strange shells rolling in his lung and eyed the breather with suspicion. The other coughed and patted his chest. Then they traded actions. Always thinking: something in this Klang is breathing wrong. I know a broken locust when I hear it. And there's one rattling inside him.

And now he makes me suck the locust-dust. Now a powdered locust-grind will dye my lining.

For the rest of days. But by then, I'll be building Egypt.

That part may be fantasy. He couldn't have predicted Egypt, could he?

So Klang slept in his boat with the moon. Lunar fingers clicked to knit him underneath their web. He slept sitting up, head lolling to the water. And thick white air, close-woven, reached above him. Put a subtle acid in his head. A thing to dry and freeze his oils, to make the ocean in his spine put creep-roots down toward the sea. The danger of the plant inside. It has to eat. Its food may scuttle with the crabs and needle-walk the lobes of closing clamshell.

When the sun came low and moonbreath broke around him, a turning net of birds jumped off the boat. They made a funnel in the wind and carved it with their feathers. As the birds revolved around their moving weather, they glanced back at Klang and knew to stay off his shoulders. Another cloud was holding him. A cloud that blackbirds know they can't escape.

The seaplain dotted with a pebble-fall of three or four dropped birds.

Hibou.

The street is now deserted of its lions.

Wind that blew off noon still feathered with their fringe. Dust still tramped to pawsmear, stone still nicked at edges with the teething of the young. But now deserted. By now no lion breath to heat the shopglass and no lion eye to catch the hunting glance from jade. Glass still fogged. Window's fibre tense where lion might've hurtled through it. Air not yet entirely slack. Still pulled around one keystring. The lion in the weave. The seacat with its horns banked at the wave. But growing looser now. The outer zone begins to rumple down. The canopy of coils above our centre, street of lions' pacing, slumps a lower hang.

Sun turned also lower. Sun's first smell of blood in hellbound boat. The long thin bark curved upward at the ends. The marble whiteness shows first cloud beneath the peeling wooden cortex. First blots in marble milk now spotted. First dim twang of sun's blood in the brain that moves the marble. In the brain that sets the wave between the wave. They smell its wound. The little cuts whose leak is afternoon. Light too ripe and ready for the bruise. Dim now. Only orange above the treeline. Only pinkish powder on the basin-lip of day. But here. Come here again to flush the coming death. We'll see. We've seen before.

Night has punched its channel through the dome.

Night's fountain readies night-stalk now. Again. Stalk of moon's dead flower and the seabound eye of moon. The marble blood in fountain veins that back the marble deathboat. Sun has set first foot into the bark.

The cold wire in my blood turns hot again.

And the street is now deserted of its lions.

The night's cat comes to steal their place. But not as lion comes. Not with heavy foot that cleaves the morning from its base. Low tide of stiff-furred breath. Low lion-flood around my warming knees. The lion comes with terror on the leash. Amazement made a volume in the muscle. That there should be a lion there; that there *is* a lion there, and every other thought become abstract. Day breaks only when the lion's sinew ripples in its coat. All before is paleness. All before is residue of night, of stillborn days, of afternoon at dawn and suns that lacked for blood.

The blanched sun has no fluid and can't feed the vent of hell. A different terror. Different from the one at lion's reins. The fraction of the hour that holds the leash. That shrinks from what's beyond its knot. That's a ghost to stay a ghost. Transparent flesh to wind around my red. My white, my blue, my glut of orange-stained pearl. The oyster in my ribs, the oyster's mother sucking tooth by tooth. Clamshell muffling heartbeat. Clamshell clapping hunger in the gut. The silent spiders clicking from the arms. The stem-walls waiting in the spinal shaft. Plant life tuned to shudder once and once be still. To know what planet rises now and know if it's a singer; to know what star should make my backbone grow and which will bomb the spine with evil rays. Before which star to shutter up the vents. Before which star to lock the leaden gate.

That's another clearness. Clearness of the leash-men. It's necessary.

Without it, I'd have no more place to hide.

But the sun that goes down bloodless is a fear. Without the drip of veins to feed our hell, the night will set off-course. Won't seat along the rims, won't take the bolt. Sun has got to roll with broken gods. There must be statue living in its sea. There must be living blood inside the fire. Some suns look more red and some more yellow. Some look white but carry all the blood. The colour's not the thing. Look at how they step into the boat. That'll tell you all about the night and how it ruins.

When sun takes awkward steps along the balding marble plank, we have not reached an end.

The death will be a mass of ragged flesh. Knives to find the ocean's bloodfed root, the sac and tendril where the ocean first arose. Knives of night will slit that sun to plies. They can't understand when there's no blood. That understanding isn't in them. Spend all night in goring out the sun, leave piles of dried out pulp to choke us. All while white moths stumble from sun's mouth. No blood to launch them nightward. All while wetless sweat drips lacquer onto hell and seals its vent.

And so, in hell, the pressure mounts and mounts.

The sun of hell, the second sun, starts beating like a heart.

No blood and then no transfer. No transfer means no talking dead. And a voiceless dead is pressure. Pressing up and out toward places of no voice. If they can't talk, the dead will climb the rootcrop. Clamber up the wheatstalk, whisper deadness to the wheat. Sound the coils of corn and mark its seed with dead-white nails. Force into the tree. Gnash at each other for the trunk. Too many dead within one brain of roots will send a fissure up the bark. Root-brain cannot think. Leaves cannot pass into their green sleep. Can't feed on green and warm the root. Too many dead inside them since the sun refused to bleed. No clear voice, no shaft of ancient song to tune the night. No seer with his blind eye toward the sea.

A voiceless dead is pressure.

The voiceless dead crawl through the wall. Sew dead vines in cement. Foundation groans. The voiceless dead will try to kill another god for blood, will hunt another blood to give them sound. Thus all the iron gods that hold up buildings; all the coral gods who hold the ocean; all the worms that grind the forest down and all the sleeping lions of the day. The lions who breathe gold between the streets. Who now are gone but come in with the sun. Unless the sun is dry and dead men choke.

Unless the sun is dry, and dead men turn to suck the lion.

So the lions have deserted, as they do. If night will roll, it rolls with other cats. And so it does. It puts me stuck among them and I stumble in their net. But that's the later part. First came the rising.

At city's edge, the vinecreep through the banks. The mud run through with gripping root. Moon now middle-raised. Its top face staring bluish at the river. City grown from river's silted crook, a maze in rings that panned for river gold. In seven rings. Each one distilled from one of seven salts; from one of seven metals that the current wraps in claws. Bottom-dragging claw to sift the sand.

And now the river's bank is breached with creeping. The carried pigments harden into veins; the carried pigments curl a vineshoot round the city's sleeping root. Mostly sleeping. But I saw it. So did cats of night. The breed that mounts the rockflat when its lions go below.

A mercury beam through black mud.

Moon-shard silver on the mercury's red face. Slow silver on the quick.

And then the second cats, in marbled red. A group of them thrust up together. Five or six. But moulded at the base. Red marble still attached them. Cat flank out of cloud-faced stone. Cat shoulder still but caught in frozen strain. The muscle rippled up around its shoulder. The lip pulled back along red marble teeth; the teeth now bare of curled red marble lip. Cat eyes redder than the rest. Ear-hollows like seafans. Like monster plants that suck the algal tide.

Still. But not silent. The stone cats' throats grown up in moulded tubes. Teeth are bared to catch the wind. To shape it into notes. Teeth shred extra harpstrings in the night-gust and maintain the marble chord. Six cats to sound the unison. To let each separate waver bob and blur; to make the chord a glass-trailed ghost borne out of humming wire.

Beneath the vine-split mud, the city's nerve is yowling.

And I yowled along. Until I was dry and silent with the song's bruise on my palate. Until I tongued its grit from my back teeth. But couldn't get inside the chord. Couldn't dive into its glassy web. I skittered on the surface, left it smudged with moon-cold sweat.

So back to the river. Back to where the blood of minerals combines. Where mixing-tide feeds metal to the flood and floodgrain to the melting edge of sky. Back in my boat and back against the planks. Back to lay against the river's roof. A boat much like the sun's, the boat that takes the sun to hell. To bleed and then to swell with blood again. A hell of draining under bloody heaven. Except that I don't know where my boat goes. I only know to wake when river shudders.

To listen for the hissing of the falls.

www.ingramcontent.com/pod-product-compliance
Lightning Source LLC
Chambersburg PA
CBHW030949090426
42737CB00007B/556